Dear Lover

Dear Lover

Edited by
SAMUEL JOHNSON OAM

Illustrated by
SHAUN TAN

hachette
AUSTRALIA

hachette
AUSTRALIA

Published in Australia and New Zealand in 2023
by Hachette Australia
(an imprint of Hachette Australia Pty Limited)
Gadigal Country, Level 17, 207 Kent Street, Sydney, NSW 2000
www.hachette.com.au

Hachette Australia acknowledges and pays our respects to the past, present and
future Traditional Owners and Custodians of Country throughout Australia and
recognises the continuation of cultural, spiritual and educational practices of
Aboriginal and Torres Strait Islander peoples. Our head office is located on the lands
of the Gadigal people of the Eora Nation.

A catalogue record for this
book is available from the
NATIONAL LIBRARY · National Library of Australia
OF AUSTRALIA

ISBN: 978 0 7336 4980 6 (hardback)

Cover and internal design by Christabella Designs
Cover and internal illustrations by Shaun Tan
Heartman illustration on pages ix and 161 by Samuel Johnson
Typeset in Garamond Regular by Kirby Jones
Printed and bound in Australia by McPherson's Printing Group

MIX
Paper | Supporting
responsible forestry
FSC
www.fsc.org   FSC® C001695

The paper this book is printed on is certified against the
Forest Stewardship Council® Standards. McPherson's
Printing Group holds FSC® chain of custody certification
SA-COC-005379. FSC® promotes environmentally
responsible, socially beneficial and economically viable
management of the world's forests.

Contents

A message from the editor

We all love differently. Some people are single by choice, some partners are dead, some prefer throuples and some people's love is well and truly on the rocks. The love we share goes up and down, and comes and goes, but when it works there's nothing like it. Even if we aren't looking for it, it can bowl us over on any given day. This collection of letters is a delightful, funny, broad and honest look at our significant others. All letters were provided free-of-charge so that more proceeds may be spent on cancer vanquishment.

Dear Lover is a stunning tribute to our loved ones, but it also helps fulfil my most longed-for wish – a cure for cancer. Cancer takes our lovers too.

Samuel Johnson OAM

Dear Lover

My darling Rebecca …

Exactly one week ago I held your hand as you safely delivered our baby girl, Margot Grace McMillan. It was nothing like the births I've seen in movies. There was no gentle breathing, no butterflies on the windowsill, and it certainly wasn't accompanied by the soothing sounds of Norah Jones.

It was long. It was traumatic. It included two failed epidurals. And it looked more like a scene from *The Texas Chainsaw Massacre*.

The colour disappeared from your face. Your entire body was shaking. You lost the ability to speak. But not for one single second did you think about giving up. You kept pushing and pushing and pushing. Using just our eyes to communicate we found a language only we understood. There may have been other people, other voices in that delivery room, but gradually they faded away. It was just you and me. The unspoken connection.

The fact is, for the majority of your twelve hours in labour you had no painkillers. I wondered how on earth you could possess such a high pain threshold. Then I remembered you'd endured two years in a relationship with me.

You were calm, strong and determined. You were always going to win. You put your body on the line for our little family and it's something I will never, ever forget. You showed me what it means to be a mum. You gave me a new level of appreciation and understanding for my mum, Loretta, and for all the mums.

I fell in love with you another hundred times that night, Rebecca. And even though this is a letter to you, I'll be cc'ing Margot because one day I want her to read it and learn all about her courageous Mumma. (I think we'll start her reading Dr Seuss and Bluey first, though – this may be a touch too graphic for a bedtime story.)

You did it. We did it. And now I've got a lifetime to try and show my immense gratitude.

Love

Sam (Dad)

Sam Mac: quick-witted weather presenter, author, radio host, mental health advocate and entertainer in the digital space who got his break when he won the SAFM 'Who Wants to Be a Co-Host on Air' competition

Dear Lover

Dear Mel,

Do you remember that day at school, in English in Year 11? Seated next to each other by demand from the teacher, mainly to stop me fooling around up the back with my mates.

How was this going to work? Embarrassing? Awkward?

I mean, we hadn't exactly spent much time working on our friendship since that little fling we had back in Year 8. The one where our first date was me taking you to the movies to see that beautiful romantic comedy called *Rambo: First Blood*!

Can't understand why that didn't work out!

That said, I'm sure I wasn't the only culprit between us not giving the relationship a chance to blossom at the age of thirteen. Remember how harsh you were in casting judgement on me for wearing my shiny blue state team tracksuit pants absolutely everywhere, perhaps even to the movies?

So, it came as quite the surprise when three years later, the thing I looked forward to most every day was that English lesson.

Remember the frustrations of the teacher, as he couldn't get us to focus because we were having too much fun sitting next to each other? Ironic, eh.

But why would I ask if you remember all these things? Of course you do. Because since that time, since that blessed day in English, when the second and continuing partnership began, you have remembered everything.

You remembered to make our wedding characteristically our own, to the point of perfection.

You remembered to encourage me to pursue my dream, instilling in me a belief in what's possible, all the while carving out your own professional career against the odds.

And as I lived out that dream, you provided the foundations and the grounding that allowed us to build a family of four gorgeous children.

Remember?

Yep, of course you do. You remember everything. Birthdays, names, holidays, kids appointments and what they want in their lunchbox for school. The uniforms, the pick-up and drop-off times. The due date for the assignment. You remember to maintain constant contact with their teachers, just to be sure. Maybe check what's going on in English!

How you remember to check on everyone else is beyond me, but you do. Friends, family and everyone else. Yet somehow, you remember to prioritise enough time for yourself to remain physically and mentally balanced in life.

This might sound odd, but I just never seem to be able to remember to do all that you do. But what I do remember is you remembering all of it my dearest friend … and I'll never, ever forget it.

For all that and more, I simply say with the most heartfelt warmth and gratitude, thank you and I love you.

Ad xxx

Adam Gilchrist: Aussie cricket legend

Dear Lover

I remember how dreamy it was just to hold hands, passionately kiss and look into each other's eyes for hours. That immense tingling sensation that I never wanted to end. That kid-like excitement knowing this was the best feeling in the world and nothing had ever felt this good before. It was new, it was intoxicating, it was naughty ... and it was so right.

After sixteen years ... it ain't like that anymore. It's BETTER!! Because this is no fleeting feeling, a passing phase or a summer fling. We know it's the real deal. Tried and true, tested over time. Like a diamond that's put under pressure to be able to sparkle in the sunlight, our relationship has been grounded by hardships, tough times and moments when I wished I'd said 'I love you' more than I did. But those times are the pressures that build diamonds and great relationships. Broken backs, career blow-ups and past traumas have ultimately made this relationship unbreakable.

The good times are easy to celebrate, but the measure of your heart is how you kept us going when the shit hit the fan. You're made of special stuff and that special stuff has been passed on to our children ... which is the greatest gift of all.

I'm not perfect, I'm a flawed human always endeavouring to do better, but it's easy to dig deeper and put in the personal work because you're worth it. We're worth it.

May the good times seriously outnumber the bad because this is still a journey that I don't ever want to end. The exact same feeling I had when I kissed you for the first time.

I can't wait to do old with you. When your tits are down between your ankles ... right next to my old-man balls. Because I'm right there beside you. For life.

Your husband

Grant xox

Grant Denyer: a man of many talents and an enthusiastic, Gold Logie-winning game-show host

Dear Lover

I never dreamt life could be so perfect. I never envisaged the depth of love I would hold in my heart for you. And for our children. I feel like my life can be summarised into two very distinct chapters: Before I met you and After I met you.

Our love is a perfect balance. Where I fall short, you lift me up. Where you fall short, I hold you. It's symmetry. Poetry. So many words in history for this type of love and yet so many people will never know a love like ours in their lifetime. And it hasn't been easy, nor has it always been smooth. We have had more than our fair share of bad times. We've experienced grief together. Tragedy. We have shared the darkest times together, trying to navigate our way through while trying to hold hands and not lose sight of one another. But, like any great romance, we have experienced monumental highs together. Our greatest achievements celebrated while arm in arm. Together.

I am grateful every day that the universe put us together when it did. It changed the entire trajectory of my life, and yours. And now looking back on that fateful day some sixteen years ago I realise that it was meant to be. Written in the stars somewhere no doubt. Two special soul mates reuniting in this life was the profundity of the connection felt. Thank you for allowing me to be myself. For showing me that being vulnerable and scared at the same time is admirable. Thank you for appreciating me for who I am. For all my faults and flaws that you adore.

But please ... stop leaving your dirty clothes on the floor.

Love

Your wife Chezzi xxx

Chezzi Denyer: Cheryl, who prefers 'Chezzi', is a freelance producer, a farmer, a mummy and an overlord with a fandangled website and a large, religious following

Dear Lover

I think you are a little more tightly wound than me, but that wouldn't be hard, because somehow I'm really relaxed now. Behind the wheel, for example. Other drivers affect you and I drive as if I'm the only car in the clouds. Speed bumps used to make you quite cross. Do you remember that? Now we play the speed bump game. We count every speed bump in any day, and we score by writing the total on masking tape, put on the dash specially. By you, of course. Our record is 36 speed bumps in one day. Speed bumps don't annoy you so much now. Now we count them together and you make me laugh when you take a detour to add to our total. Now speed bumps are our friends.

We duel. Conflict is at the heart of every story and our life is a story. But because we don't fight or argue we have to invent conflict. So we play Yahtzee. Our current Yahtzee score is 394 (you) and 368 (me). You are superior in so many more ways though. Don't get me wrong, I cut my weight and I'm better at tennis and floors and chopping wood and carrying stuff, but you do life so well and I admire that. I hope we can play hundreds more games of Yahtzee. I hope my score never catches yours.

This is a crazy world. A curveball to the temple can strike on any idle Tuesday and throw everything upside down. None of us are immune. Sometimes life happens. All I hope is that I can hold hands with someone and walk through the world with them, curveballs and all. You are that person. You hold my hand. And you agree with me – not to be a cunt. Ever. And you're really good in the kitchen. That helps. I'm joking, obviously. I just wanted to squiggle this quick note for you. This letter is not hard, because I knew what it boiled down to from the start. Thanks for holding my hand and counting speed bumps with me. I hope you live longer than me because I don't want to watch you die, which is the only way I could lose you.

x Sam

PS Now you owe me a love letter too!

Samuel Johnson: cancer vanquisher, dee-lebrity and proud brother

Dear Lover

Well, I don't know where to start. I haven't had a lover in a while, so this has come as a little bit of a shock! It's all happening so fast.

My love life before you has been a little bit tragic. 'Unlucky in love', they say. I like to think I'm just waiting for Prince Charming to come along. Or Crocodile Dundee. Whatever.

To be completely honest, life as a senator can be a bit lonely. I'm always on the move, which makes it difficult to hold down a relationship. But I'm learning to make time for me, and you'll be a big part of that.

There's some things you should probably know, if we're going to take this any further.

Rules for dating Jacqui Lambie:
- You've got to like Dagwood Dogs.
- You will constantly be picking up half-drunk water bottles from around the house.
- Don't judge me for reading a Jackie Collins book.

- I will judge you on your driving. I drove army trucks, what do you expect?
- Must love *Rambo*. Non-negotiable.
- I put my tea bags in the kitchen sink when I'm done.
- Put up with the 12 a.m. phone calls from veterans.
- Know that you share me with 500 000 Tasmanians.
- Let me make this clear – I don't have time for silly buggers. Having a lover sure is nice, but I'm okay on my own. I'm used to it.

If this hasn't scared you off, well let's get to it, baby! Write back soon okay?

Love

Jacqui

Jacqui Lambie: former Australian Defence Force soldier, Tasmanian senator and participant in Season 5 of I'm a Celebrity … Get Me Out of Here!

Dear Lover

Take me back to the first time, before –
fairy lights in dark pub corners pool tables backyard parties
    fire buckets in the night
across a beach a river a picnic across a table full of empty pot
    glasses across the dance floor on the
sticky green carpet at the Punters Club the jangle of nerve
    endings sparking
like there is phosphorescence glittering crazy between us and
    eye contact like a
drum beat da DUM da DUM until there is no stopping it
    inevitable that loose-limbed falling into something that is
    altogether not of this world

someone should bottle this

this moment this limerence this beforeness this anticipation
this chemical skin heart alchemy you could keep it always,
high on a shelf like the BFG does with those dreams – the

good ones – all luminous colour ballooning and blossoming –
take it out and sniff it, lick it, light it, hold it close

hold

the bit on the screen that makes the kids squeal now, the
squirm of delight the knowing it's coming the leaning in closer
and closer and did you know there are more than one million
nerve endings in your lips?

and we kiss
and we kiss
and we kiss
you know I fall hard for the past
always crushing on nostalgia
do you remember?
falling in love that first time

on a highway your hand on my knee my feet on the dash the
white line rushing through the rust hole in the floor

 xx

Kate Mildenhall: author of Skylarking *and* The Mother Fault,
and co-host of The First Time *podcast*

Dear Lover

I hope this finds you well.

I am writing to inform you that from now on, I will turn my computer off at 5 p.m.

If you miss me, please know that I am trying not to think of you.

Last night you stole the sheets again. I dreamt of empty white pages and blinking cursors. I woke to you asking for more more more. At breakfast this morning, we spoke in constructive feedback. I buttered my toast with product reviews. I sweetened my coffee with keywords. Don't get me wrong, I appreciate you – really – but I need some space.

No more late-night word count. No more red squiggly underlines. No more 'making things work'.

Do you understand? I'm worn out. I love you but it's complicated.

Take care, my love.

Sincerely

Freelance Writer

Jodelle Marx: spoken word poet from Oregon, USA, who currently lives and works at an artist residency in Italy

Dear Lover

It's been a wild ride and I really don't know where to start this letter ...

At the beginning? I'll never forget that night Charlie Pickering introduced us in the back room at The Fox Hotel in Collingwood. I remember exactly where I was standing and I remember exactly how you made me feel. I was so drawn to you, I felt an immediate connection, a buzz inside that I hadn't felt for so long. You were so cool. We chatted, we flirted and we snuck off onto the street for a first kiss ... not realising that we were standing outside a window and everyone in the pub could watch on and enjoy the moment. And if they missed the moment, they would have seen the red lipstick smeared all over my face.

A moment revisited in *New Idea* when they secretly photographed our wedding and went with the headline 'You May Now Smudge the Bride' and there I was with red lipstick smeared all over my face four years after that first meeting.

Technically you still haven't said 'yes' to my lengthy proposal but I guess it's a moot point now. You did say 'Why are you saying these things?', 'I don't know what's going on', 'This is weird' and my personal favourite, 'Are you testing comedy material?' You eventually closed with 'Holy snapping duckshit you're fucking serious', which I took as a 'yes'.

We bonded over the movie *True Romance*, good food, good wine, fun holidays, a hatred of Donald Trump and a love of animals.

You have endured my undying love of the Hawthorn Football Club and I have sat through hundreds of hours of *RuPaul's Drag Race*.

You introduced me to your little girls – Tama and Sachi – and I fell in love immediately. I was never a cat person but those two little treasures converted me. Even on those nights (too many nights) when they decided to sleep on my head, or my chest or my legs, I never wavered.

But our two greatest achievements are … our rescue Staffy, Bunny. She has brought us so much joy together and is a part of our family as much as any human could be. Despite sleeping on the bed and eating chocolate and vomiting on the good rug we couldn't love her any more. Your love of animals and advocacy for animal rights groups is one of your most endearing qualities.

And our wee man, the Ladster, Laddie Buster Lehmann. You are such an amazing mum. I see how he loves you and how much you love him in return, and it makes me want to burst into tears like I did in the delivery suite when I laid eyes on him for the first time. Even when he climbs into our bed at 3 a.m. I couldn't love him any more!

Yes there are five in the bed but that's cool, we are one big, mixed, wild family … that needs a bigger bed.

I love you until the end of days.

Your husband,

Lehmo xx

Lehmo: one of Australia's most well-travelled comedians who has completed seven 'tours of duty' performing for troops abroad. Once held the Guinness World Record for the most jokes told in an hour (549)

Dear Lover

I'll never forget waking up next to you, your eyes were already open, watching me. I quickly covered my face with my hands. Scared you would see all my imperfections. The ones people who had claimed to love me in the past had pointed out.

You gently took my hands away and looked into my eyes. You told me I was beautiful. And I could feel what you meant. You meant I was beautiful to you. In spite of any imperfections. To you, they were perfect. To you, I was perfect.

You saw me, the good and bad, and you loved it all. It wasn't always pretty and it didn't have to be. You didn't expect the perfectionism from me that I expected from myself.

The way you held my hand as we crossed the road, held the small of my back when we stood in line, put your arm around me sitting at the table. I felt protected and safe in a way that has never left.

Fifteen years later and we have been by each other's side the whole time. Life has been generous – throwing us many amazing, wonderful experiences and evening them out with the difficult ones to remind us to never stop being grateful.

The day our son was born, our relationship as lovers took a slight detour. Because there was someone who needed us more than we needed each other. But as time passes (and we have more sleep) I see us finding our way back to those young lovers who met and fell head over heels in love. But now we are older and wiser. And I have seen your loyalty, strong morals, kindness, generosity and heart at work for many years. So if it's possible – I love you more now than I ever did.

Christie

Christie Whelan Browne: doyen of musical theatre, #MeToo champion and keeper of so many awards that she pants when she tries to carry them all

Dear Lover

As soon as I finish writing this, the first thing I'll want to do is give it to you to look over. I value your opinion so much, I can barely send a fucking text without asking for your input.

BUT, I'll have to fend (edit) for myself on this occasion, as we are both contributing to this book and I want the first time you read this to be when you hold a copy in your hands, and flip through all the other love letters to get to ours.

Hold on.

What if you write a 'Dear Lover' letter to someone else?

Shit.

That would be fucking hilarious.

And tremendously awkward.

Ha.

I kinda hope you do.

Because then I could hold it over you for the rest of our days. It'd be here in black and white – me, the good person, and you, the guy who wrote a love letter to someone other than his wife.

It's not a competition or anything, and you know I don't have a competitive bone in my body, but I'd definitely be the winner.

I mean, if anyone other than you actually bothers to read this, they'd have to agree.

They'd also likely think I was a complete nut.

And you know that I am.

See, that's the thing about us, we are exactly the same brand of silly.

When I first told people we'd started seeing each other, their standard reaction was 'Oh, yay!!' rapidly followed by, 'That makes so much sense'.

I don't think I'd fully made sense before us.

And not in a 'you complete me' soppy rom-com kinda way (which might be a not-so-secret guilty pleasure of mine). More in a 'I've sorted out a bunch of my shit now, and this relationship just works in a way I never imagined one could' kinda way.

It's all about timing isn't it?

And learning.

I learnt a lot from relationships past:

How-to.

How-definitely-not-to.

How RuPaul is one wise-ass drag queen when she says at the end of each episode of *Drag Race*, 'If you can't love yourself, how in the hell are you going to love somebody else?'

Amen!

Okay, so now I've spent the best part of this letter being a complete twit and quoting a TV show.

BUT! I don't need to worry. I get to tell you every day exactly why I love you, because nothing is ever left unsaid between us, and that is something I am extremely proud of.

Thank you for that.

For always saying all the things.

Because of you and your love, I feel safe. I feel supported. I feel capable in the world.

And that's all I need.

You are my EVERYTHING, Toby.

Don't die before me.

X Michala

(PS If you had edited this, it would have been a million times better than this hot mess. Fact.)

*Michala Banas: actor (*Upper Middle Bogan, McLeod's Daughters*), sometime singer, sometime chocolate over-eater, lover of laughter, married to Toby Truslove*

Dear Lover

This is awkward. You've just sent me to the office to write this very letter. It's Sunday and I'm usually destroying the kitchen cooking pancakes. You've already written your letter like a tiny swot, and I promised to do mine weeks ago and then promptly forgot.

You're good like that. The brains of the operation. My better half. That's a funny old phrase but I think it says a lot. For me it says that with you, I am more than I was by myself. An addition of one to one that somehow produces more than two. It's a strange alchemy. My better half. It's actually sweet to say. Better. Half. Because you are better than me at a lot of things. I don't mind. I love it. And you care enough to want me to be better too. That's the kicker, I think. Better, not for you, but for me, for my happiness, my equilibrium. Making me better at exposing to the light all the bits I sometimes want to hide in the dark. At ignoring the dumb stoic streak that runs through my family and share with you everything I am, good bad indifferent. You being better makes me better. A better man, better husband, better brother, son, uncle, friend, stranger. So there it is. I love you. Utterly. Always.

Better-er each day. Now it's time to make pancakes. I make pancakes better than you.

I'll mess up the kitchen, you'll make it better.

Love

Toby

Toby Truslove: 'go to' comedic Australian TV and stage actor, married to Michala Banas

Dear Lover

The mind whirrs and the past flashes behind the eyes like a slide show on speed when you're asked to write a letter to your lover. Loved lovers, liked lovers, lovers with unknown names, lovers that could have been, lovers that shouldn't have been, forgotten lovers, never-quite-forgotten lovers.

Then there's the dilemma of who to write to. Do I address a regret? The thought is gone before it begins. Obviously, you have to write to your current lover, or you may find yourself single again. Unless a previous lover has passed away, then the current lover has to support the letter to the ex. Anyway, this behind-the-scenes exposé is putting off the inevitable.

There has been one, long, undying love. My friend, my confidante, you've been there without judgement. We go places together, we build magic everywhere we go, you're always there, even when I'm not. Sure, you make yourself known, leave bits of yourself and little unobtrusive signs around the place to remind me that you're there when I'm less attentive. But you never complain when I go off with my friends, go to places without you, or even when I forget about you altogether for a time. Your colourful, bright and reliable personality is always there when I get back. I love you, Lego. And I was going to write this letter to you. A thank you, if you will, for your loyalty, your friendship, your guidance. When I spend time with you, my perspective returns. You make me … well, *me*.

But I met someone else. And this letter is for her. You both coexist in my life, you stay out of each other's way. There are even times when my person sends me your way to find my calm. She accepts you, and she'll never come between us – we have her permission. Come to think of it, you haven't really opened up to me about how you feel about her. Were you trying to send a message when I stepped on a piece of you in the middle of the night last week? Surely not. It's not how you operate.

So here goes.

Dear Lover,

A couple of years ago, I wanted to do something nice for an amazing friend. I wanted to write her a letter; a thank you letter. And I thought it would be wonderful if I got her family and friends to write one too. A book of letters from those she loved, from those she's helped along the way. But I'm a dreadful stalker. I couldn't find anyone connected to her through social media. I drew blanks everywhere I turned. Someone suggested I try you, dear Lover. You were her friend too. For six days and six nights we amassed letters and swapped stories into the wee hours. There was no consequence to us being all of ourselves. We were finite. There was an end date. No shame. No judgement.

Except I was already in love with you.

When the borders dropped, I invited myself to your house for six days. And there you were. Your front steps were almost insurmountable ... your face took my air away. After some mini-adventures, I headed back to life. We talked every spare minute and word came. The borders were going up again. You printed a permit, hopped in your car, and made it through with minutes to spare. To fourteen days iso with me and my family, who you'd never met. Your fierceness and natural courage are some of my favourite things. It's all my favourite, come to think of it.

But looking across pillows at your face at the end of the day, and chattering away like we haven't seen each other for a year is my favourite favourite. So is the way you put your warrior on when you think I've been slighted; the way you think everything is terrific, even little average things; how you get so excited about the day ahead; how wherever we go is more special than before you. Your curiosity, your enthusiasm. The way you talk like we're forever. It's all my favourite favourite.

Even more favourite than Lego ... but let's keep that detail between ourselves.

Hildegaard

Hilde Hinton: author, prison officer, Love Your Sister co-founder and proud owner of bright red hair

Dear Lover

I can't quite believe it's been 22 years. Far out! All that time ago, when you were the lighting dude at The Espy and I was the new comic. You were just 'that guy' with the long hair and rock and roll good looks that my seven-year-old son Abel wouldn't shut up about. 'Mum, Mum you should talk to Tony, please, he's a nice man, he gave me a balloon last Sunday when you were on stage.' So I checked you out on his insistence. I could tell from your nervousness that you might have had a bit of a crush. Especially when after having a conversation with me you turned around and walked into a wall. That was pretty much a sign that you were crushing on me.

So ... after all this time, here we are ... still together, married, with a beautiful daughter together and a (step)son you helped raise.

We have Real Estate, money in the bank, both our careers are in a good place etc. etc., but we find ourselves in a conundrum. We've lost the spark. I can't fucking figure it out, and neither can you. Is it because of being worn down over time? Is it possible there were too many dramas? One too many lockdowns, one too many arguments, one too many deaths and illnesses? I don't bloody know.

I was thinking maybe we should do what my sister and her husband do, and go on a regular date night, that might fix things. Or I've heard that most long-term relationships will just coast every now and then. Maybe when we're in Thailand we can find some time to be romantic.

We could try counselling again.

Look, it's not that I don't love you, but I just don't like some things about you. I don't like being blamed, or feeling guilty or like I'm in trouble. This is what I reckon has happened. I reckon we stopped being lovers, the lovers we were when we first met. We started being partners. Which includes a lot of admin. There's so much to it really. Housekeeping, finance, education, health. There's so much bloody admin.

So, let's try to say hello to each other every day. Properly, with a hug and a kiss. Before we start on all the day-to-day information and whether we need bread and milk and who has what appointment blah blah blah. Let's stop and say hello to each other. Let's take each other in. Let's be fascinated with each other again. Let's act as if we don't know what the other is going to do next. Let's surprise each other. Let's go out. Just the two of us. Maybe we can go to The Espy. We could have a reminisce. We could be in the same building where it (we) all began.

I'll do the admin and make a booking.

Looking forward to our date night

Bev xxxxx

Bev Killick: bold, brassy and overly likeable, Bev is a stand-up comic and actor who includes cruise ships and Puppetry of the Penis *tours amongst her many exploits*

Dear Lover

That shit you did in bed was crazy and I loved it. I had never seen anybody do the things that you did and I never have since. Is that stuff legal?

That night is a memory I will never forget (I had never seen equipment and dexterity like that before) but it wasn't just the sex ... it was much more to me and hopefully you.

As I remember, the next morning I had to travel 300 kilometres to the next gig and threw up out the window of a BMW for 57 kilometres of that drive. It was worth it!

I didn't really get to know you well, but I felt we had good chemistry and a great connection. Who knows, if we had been in the right place at the right time, maybe things would have turned out differently.

Maybe we would have got married and had kids together. I guess it just wasn't meant to be.

Years later, I tried to track you down to see if we could rekindle our relationship but only knowing your name as Bubbles made this impossible.

An unreliable source told me you got married and made little bubbles – apparently it was a water birth. An even more unreliable source suggested that you had become a nun. I found this ridiculous at first but then I remembered how often you yelled 'Oh God' on that fateful night.

Either way, I hope you are happy with your family ... or God?

You are the one that got away. If only you had told me your real name instead of 'call me Bubbles' maybe we would have lived happily ever after.

That didn't happen but it is a night I will never forget, and I thank you for a spectacular effort and performance!

I truly hope life has treated you as well as you treated me on that lusty night in the '80s.

Give your kids a hug for me or probably better – ask God to pray for me!

Thank you Bubbles!

Brian xx

Brian Mannix: actor, author, radio presenter, energetic frontman of '80s band Uncanny X-Men and winner of Mr Ocean Grove in 1971

Dear Lover

To quote the title of a song made famous by my old friend Jon English, 'words are not enough'.

We've been together for a long, long time. The love you show for me is truly unbelievable; I could never have had such a successful career without your guidance and love; when times were tough you never wavered, you are always there for me.

In my eyes, you are the perfect mother and grandmother for our family. Everyone loves you, they love your wicked sense of humour, your impeccable taste, your generosity, your attention to detail and your self-taught awareness of the weird and crazy world we live in.

There have been times in my life when I thought that everything was turning sour; you were and always are there to rescue me.

In these later years of our lives with the onset of health problems and more pills than a chemist shop, it's you that reminds me of my daily schedule. You never fail me.

There have been some challenging issues that we've had to deal with over the years, some very recently – every time I'm left in awe at the way you handle these situations.

This poor schmuck doesn't deserve the love and care that you freely give to me.

I love you, I always have and I always will.

John

John Paul 'King of Pop' Young: an Australian music industry elite who has amassed over 4 million record sales since the '70s as well as a bunch of awards and a spot in the ARIA Hall of Fame

Dear Lover

By the time you read this, I will be dead. No, I won't! Well, I certainly hope I'm not dead. I don't want this to be a tragic love story. But that would just be my luck to jest about dying in a love letter to you and then to actually die before you read it so it becomes some kind of sick joke. Man, I really hope I'm not dead. I don't know why I started this letter like that. Probably to make you laugh? I hope you're laughing and I hope I'm alive when you read this.

The funny thing is, as I'm writing this at my kitchen table with the traffic outside blaring and my next-door neighbour almost definitely engaged in a drug deal, I've actually never felt more alive because we have just fallen in love. Not *just* but very recently in the grand scheme of things. Part of me wishes it had happened sooner because (ready for the really soppy part?) before you, I thought that love had forgotten about me. I felt like I had become the punchline to a joke that I was sick of telling. Before you, even when I was with someone, I felt lonely. But not anymore. No one has ever loved me like you do and I've never been happier than when I'm just holding your hand or laughing with you at the stupid things that make us laugh.

Our love story, like all great love stories, began with a lack of chairs. And I hope that I'm sitting next to you for a very long time. For the rest of time, actually.

I love you. Probably more.

Love

Susan

PS You better check for a pulse. Just in case.

Susie Youssef: comedian, actor, writer and TV panel regular

Dear Lover

Do not attempt my rescue, should I fly away thru fear
Be lenient with my trembling heart, respect my anxious tears
And should I fall, I beg of you, please slowly turn away
For I will pass as seasons pass, forgiving loves decay

You led me to your garden and surrendering to you
I lost control along the way, as lovers often do
But seasons pass as winter plays, your garden fades to grey
For I will pass as seasons pass, forgiving loves decay

If love's too much of a sacrifice, so much more of a sacrifice
Unless the winter brings a change of heart, I'll sacrifice
    my soul
Cos winter darkness could not foresee
That winter gave love to you and me
I'll leave your garden when the music dies
That's the irony of love

And should I fall I beg of you, please slowly turn away
For I will pass as seasons pass forgiving loves decay
I will be forgiving loves decay ...
Tell me what more can I say

I have nothing left to give.

Jeff

Jeff Duff: flamboyant entertainer extraordinaire who has released a whopping 27 albums

Dear Lover

Initially, I was going to write this letter to you, my beloved, using my trademark wit and humour.

In other words, I was gonna take the piss.

I would start it off with a list, something to engage the reader, like '10 Things I Hate About My Valentine'.

1. He leaves toothpaste residue in the sink.
2. His dress sense can be somewhat … lacking.
3. If I say 'Michael!' he won't say anything back, which leads me to say 'MICHAELLLLL!' even louder. To which he will say 'I heard you' and I'll say 'Well you didn't say anything back'. It's not a very empowering interaction. 😄
4. He's nice to everyone. I mean, this is ostensibly a great quality, but it does mean he says hello to literally everyone on the street, and inquires about how their renovations are going and if the health of their goldfish has improved since switching to organic fish food. Quick trips to town? Yeah, not possible with Michael.

But then I realised I was trying to make our relationship seem funny and sarcastic when, in reality, it's the exact opposite.

If I'm being honest, it's hard for me to admit how much someone means to me, because I'm worried that I could lose them, and who wants to be with someone desperate?

But if there's one thing I'm trying to teach my sons, it's to say how you feel, and to tell the people you love how much you love them.

So.

Dear Beloved Michael, father of my children, I love you.

You are the nicest, kindest, humblest, most self-effacing human that I have ever met, and being with you has made me a better person.

I think the first time I knew I had a crush on you was when I was twelve and I went into Tuckerbag and you were stacking shelves.

Then you went on a date with one of my friends and I was jealous.

Then there was that time at a party when you came back to my house but you just passed out in my bed.

Then there was that other time when I had my 21st and you came and I was hoping you'd sleep in my bed but you went home.

Then there were those times when we almost pashed but didn't, almost slept together but didn't.

Almost.

Almost.

Almost.

Almost.

Until one day I got annoyed, and thought, *That's it, if Michael Hoskin is at the party tonight I will kiss him.*

And you were there, and we did kiss, and I hate all that bullshit about first kisses but I swear our first kiss felt like a Wizz Fizz up my back and like stars were exploding in my eyes.

What came next? Predictable. We dated, had fun, went surfing, went running, had adventures, I got a job as an engineer in WA and you came with me, and our whole lives stretched out in front of us like an empty Western Highway.

And then?

We became unpredictable.

I got seriously injured, badly burned while running in an ultramarathon.

And you were with me every morning in hospital and every evening in hospital. You would tuck me in and tell me you loved me and you were proud of me and that you would see me in the morning.

Day after day, week after week, month after month, countless kilometres driven in your blue Holden Commodore station wagon to endless appointments and doctors and surgeries and meetings and pain.

And rinse and repeat, rinse and repeat.

Because of you, and your love, and your support and your care, I knew that whenever I faltered or whenever I was unsure I could always rely on you.

I only have the life I have today because of you, and I am only the person I am today because of you, and I can be the mother I want to be because of you.

My story is our story, and it's the story of two young people who were thrown into a hellhole but somehow made it out with their love intact.

The story of two people who get to have a family together and keep living life and keep having adventures.

Like I said. Unpredictable.

I love you.

Turia Pitt: bestselling author, athlete and mindset coach

Dear Lover

If I were a dog,
My tail would not stop wagging,
All because of you.
(a haiku)

Jeremy

Jeremy Lachlan: author, gay, adorable, currently single

Dear Lover

Actually 'Lover' just doesn't sound quite right for the person that I love so much.

Let me rephrase that ...

Dear Love of my life ... my Raquel.

You know I really do believe you are actually magic ... just like the genie in a bottle with the wishes etc. I know because I've been keeping track. I also know I'd better be careful what I wish for. I really think the difference between magic and manifestation is just a matter of the time that passes between the wish and fruition.

It seems like magic just follows you around.

Remember when we were riding our Triumph through the forest, and that beautiful white horse appeared out of nowhere and started galloping along next to us ... that was magic.

And that time we were driving down Long Gully Road and all those deer appeared out of the woods ... that was definitely magic.

And anytime when things have seemed hopeless, it's always worked out in the end. Magic.

But I don't just love you because of your magic. Don't get me wrong, I love the magic, it's just that there are many other things I love about you too.

I love that your favourite car is a Ferrero Rocher.

I love that you met a man who walked on the moon.

I love that you are not afraid of spiders.

I love the way that you'll sometimes just start trying to open the door of some random car, thinking it's ours.

I love the way you always shield me from our microwave oven, even though I tell you that's how I get my superpowers.

Oh yeah, and I love the way you exercise in high heels.

But most of all I love the way you love me … that … and the magic.

Which brings me to my quest … it's about the wishes.

I really do have a wish, and I think you know what it is.

Remember 'the bird that rose from the ashes'?

I love you ♥

Brizee x

Brian Canham: founding member of the iconic Pseudo Echo and Countdown*'s 'Most Popular Male Performer'*

Dear Lover

Do you ever wonder sometimes about … why you and why me? How a little boy growing up in the hustle and bustle of inner Sydney would someday cross paths with a little girl from a farm in the Mallee, Vic. Was it fate or in the stars or did the angels help … were we meant to be, all along? I can hear you now saying, 'That's the storyteller you' … but I often wonder about this and whether there were angels giving us a little shove in the right direction. When I hear of great loves coming to an end, I think could this ever be us? Here, right now, I say we are *forever* and I can't see it any other way. To think of losing you, for whatever reason, ignites the start of heartache, so let's change the subject.

What I love about you most is the way you treat me and our boys. We always feel so safe and top priority. I love that you mow the lawns (so I don't have to) and fix things I cannot. I love that you always encourage me to sing even when I start to doubt myself. When I stop singing my leaves start to wilt. Your encouragement is like throwing blood and bone on me.

You know deep down it makes me happy ... simple ... black and white.

Just so you know, I never get tired of seeing you every day. I never get tired of having my first coffee with you in the morning or a red wine at night. Most of all ... I never tire watching you love and raise our boys. Crossing paths or stars aligning or angels' help ... I met my 'one of a kind'.

Love

Me x

Sara Storer: multi-Golden Guitar-awarded singer–songwriter who feels motivated when it rains

Dear Lover

I fell into your world, literally. I was drunk, broke a finger and subsequently lost my wallet, a shoe and a packet of Fisherman's Friends lozenges along the way. The latter, after reeking of the midnight kebab, was a devastating loss and those who came across my breath that night would have considered a zesty breath mint blessed relief, or so you said.

I don't remember the taxi drive or the emergency room shenanigans involving the other wounded drunk people but I remember your perfumed scent, which you told me later didn't exist as you never wore perfume. Perhaps it was the taxi driver or the triage nurse?

Your first intimate glimpse of me was my bare bum through the hospital gown, lucky you, and mine of you, your neck, when we first met. No, I don't have a fetish for necks in particular. It's just that I considered the small necklace you wore infinitely lucky to be on such a beautiful patch of skin.

Anyhow, I know you told me all those years ago that writing letters is reserved for old men in cardigans but considering my age now, the time in-between drinks and (ahem) my warm cardigan, it seems fitting, as does the cardigan.

Time doesn't heal the gravity of such loss although I know that you are not entirely gone, sure, your heart doesn't beat anymore but mine beats faster when I think of you so, somehow, somewhere, you are connecting with me.

I'm perpetually angry that you didn't wear perfume! Your scent, left on the clothes I have of yours, would have been comforting to me as I lie here in a similarly inebriated state as I was when we first met!

See you very soon xx

Damon

Damon Smith: musician, ballet composer, cabaret writer and a creator who is prolific for his work in the realm of mental illness

Dear Lover

To express in a letter my love for you. What a challenge to originality to express an amorphous sense that we all experience, all know, all seek and all attempt to express.

To speak of how I feel when I see you, think of you, touch your hand, hear your voice, hear your name. How it feels like my stomach is smiling. How do I say any of this?

Make it funny? 'I love you, now here's a joke.' Maybe not. Doesn't really carry the gravitas I'm searching for.

Make it beautiful. Well, the great poets, writers, storytellers and creators have done this for as long as we've been sentient. How do I compete with them?

Maybe just artlessly quote past geniuses. Trawl through the sonnets of Shakespeare, the glorious beauty of Shelley or Tennyson. Copy and paste. It certainly shows I care and unquestionably gets the message across, but 'I love you so much I stole someone else's words' – not what I'm going for today.

Perchance I could clothe my language with occasional past phrasing to transport you to bygone times and provide an illusion of inventiveness. All the while searching for that perfect esoteric line buried deep within a little-known song, book or film. The words that carry the lyrical soul of my purpose – 'I love you so much that I stole someone else's words, but I did look really hard for them.' Nah …

So, I come to this. A short missive around my experience, with you and through you. Of love and confrontation and confusion and fear and sadness and grief and happiness and joy and, well … Everything.

Because you turned my life of ignorant privilege inside out. I may well have thought I was happy if a sliding-door moment had left you unmet, but no.

Something was missing. Not right. The hole that was there before you, that I ignored, that I self-medicated my way around, would have continued to gnaw. That's gone now.

I fought. Oh, how I fought. Because I knew better. I was right. I knew me. How dare you. You're not the boss of me.

All whilst knowing full well that I was wrong. Another cowardly lion on the yellow-brick-road of life. Reading stridently from *The Book of Men*.

The infinitesimally small chance that led to a random collection of stardust taking shape to form me, fill it with whatever life is, and become aware of itself, was being wasted. And still you stood there, hand outstretched, saying, 'Come on. Join us at the grown-up's table. Be happy.'

I used to be embarrassed and angry. I used to be unable to handle the grief of my waste. I used to struggle with unnamed sadness. I used to lie to myself and others. I used to hurt others. And I'd roll through this self-destructive cycle over and over again.

And all the while, you'd be there. Calm, kind, forgiving,

understanding and, above all, loving. Always being the example I could follow anytime I chose. Seeing what I didn't even want to look at and patiently waiting because hey, everyone has their own journey, and their own path don't they? You showed me that, and that none of us have the right to tell another what to do or be or feel because you lived it.

I remember telling someone once a version of this story, telling them how I felt about you. Of the gifts you had shown me.

Their cynicism gland was fully formed, and they laughed and reminded me that all we feel that makes us happy is the production of chemicals in our bodies. Not real emotions, just these chemicals that give us the illusion of feeling.

But how wonderful is it that I got to meet you? Someone who produces these chemicals in my body. How amazing is it that I met someone who helped me experience feeling this way? How astonishing is that?

And to do it in the face of what I was. To see through that. To see what lay beneath and stay and work and love and love and love.

That's real. That's not an illusion. So, for being someone I love and who loves me, thank you. For the love and confrontation and confusion and fear and sadness and grief and happiness and joy and, well … Everything. Because, with you, everything is wonderful.

Lots of love

Joel

Joel Bryant: actor, stand-up comic, Roller Derby announcer and the Orange County Fair pie-eating champion

Dear Lover

I found all the letters you wrote me the other day. They were under the house in a box with some old postcards. I struggled with some of the names scrawled on the cards, but I hadn't forgotten you.

The letters were bundled in a rubber band which had long withered with age. I hadn't realised you'd sent so many.

They had been opened but I had long forgotten their contents.

Your neat handwriting was faint on the page, like you hadn't pushed the pen too hard, but the words remained. They hit me like a ton of bricks.

Reading and re-reading took me back to Year 10. You were sitting at the back of the school bus: loud, obnoxious and so very funny.

I liked you instantly.

You'd been thrown out of your last school, now here you were at ours. It was obvious you didn't conform and you didn't give a shit about what people thought about you. There was also something almost punk rock about you when compared to the other boys in the class. They were dull. You were dangerous.

I suppose I was flattered that you flirted with me. I felt special. It validated me in that class full of clowns.

The other kids gossiped. I wasn't like the other girls. I didn't concern myself with silly games and bitchy name-calling. I was an outsider.

'I like you cos you're not like them,' you'd tell me. 'They're so busy worrying about how they appear to everyone else, that they're not themselves. They're all fake. You're real.'

We wagged school together and watched daytime TV on your sofa whilst your parents were working. We went to Coles and you nicked two cans of Fanta and popped them down your trackies. I was shocked but impressed. Rebel.

Mum was also impressed when you came to pick me up to take me to the movies. 'I'll have her back before 11 p.m., Mrs Gazzo.'

That was the night we snogged in the back row and played pinball on Bourke Street.

I got nervous when you held my hand. All these new feelings. Your company was intoxicating.

I hadn't met anyone like you.

You had a way of looking at the world that blew my mind.

I know the other girls wondered why me and not them. I was the chosen one. I felt lucky.

It took me weeks to find the right dress for the end of year dance.

When you asked me to be your date, my heart leapt. I had never been to a formal before. I chose black. So very teenage goth of me.

We were a few days out from the big night when one of those school bitches sat next to me in art class.

She informed me with a catty tone that you were taking *her* to the formal.

I knew she was full of shit. You wouldn't be seen dead with a fake chick with orange tan.

'Oh didn't you know? He's not taking you anymore. He asked me to go with him. Sorry!'

The other orange-tanned girls around her all nodded in unison. They were smiling. I couldn't work out if it was a bad joke.

I looked at you and you didn't need to say anything. Your face said it all.

The sky fell in.

My world collapsed around me.

Tongues wagged and fingers pointed.

I called you at home.

Through tears I managed to muster the sentence, 'If you didn't want to take me to the formal you could have told me to my face!'

Silence from you.

I hung up.

I never spoke to you again.

The following year I enrolled in a new school. No Jane could survive in that dumb old school full of Heathers anyway.

I ignored the letters you sent to my house.

I moved on.

It was surreal finding those letters recently. In them you apologised profusely and asked if we could be friends again.

There was genuine sincerity.

I had a good cry as I read and re-read those words written over 30 years ago. You reiterated that you loved my individuality because I was unlike everyone else.

And I guess that's why I was so heartbroken.

When you dumped me for her, you had become exactly like them.

Jane

Jane Gazzo: radio broadcaster, author, MC, co-host of '90s cult TV show Recovery, *and former teenage goth and sentimentalist*

Dear Lover

If I called you 'Lover' you would stomp on my foot. Gently, but enough that I'd get the message.

If I declared my undying love in fancy prose, your eyes would roll back so far in your head I'd wonder if they were coming back.

If I wrote about our possible futures, you would remind me that I can barely tie my shoelaces properly, let alone predict the future.

If I wrote you a letter and shared it with people, you wouldn't forgive me.

If I singled you out in a crowd to thank you, you would run out of the room.

You can see the dilemma I'm in.

So I'm not going to write about the places we've been, those particular skies, rivers, currents and clouds. I won't write about bookshops and foggy summer evenings in cities I didn't know. I won't write about balancing our equation. I won't write about the time you … when I … or that you are the most ... I won't write about finding home. I won't write about knowing. I won't write about being so glad that in this crumbling, sparkling world that we have been, and we are.

I'd prefer we keep it between ourselves too.

Rhett

Rhett Davis: writer of fiction that sits somewhere between the real and the unreal

Dear Lover

How exciting to experience true joy, happiness and partnership. To know that we create our own future; that we are committed to each other's wellbeing; that our future selves will know wellness, learning, discovery, connection, giving and recognition together.

I am so grateful to you for creating such a safe space for us and that we are able to be, say and act as our authentic selves. We are real, open and care deeply. We can say what needs to be said, do what needs to be done and create the community and family around us that supports our endeavours and who we are as a couple and as a family. We are truly together, we never need to be alone – we have each other's backs (fronts, sides and ups and downs).

I am excited to share my dreams, and to make them a reality with you. To plan, explore and discover. I love how we create a theme which helps to guide us each year. Our conversations are rich, interesting and full of curiosity.

I am forever thankful that we found each other. Every day I wake up next to you, bursting with excitement about the discussions we will have, and the adventures we will be on together that day, and the next and next and next.

I see you, I know you, I love you.

Thank you for being the love of my life.

Naomi

Naomi Simson: entrepreneur, business leader, author, RedBalloon founder, Big Red Group co-founder and the Red Shark on Shark Tank Australia. *Cerebral Palsy Research Foundation board member. Married to her soul mate, Stuart King*

Dear Lover

What can I say?

The past 32 years in your wonderful company have been fun, loving, passionate at times – particularly when conceiving the children (winking emoji) – and I cannot imagine anyone else tolerating my control freak, mercurial tendencies. Mind you, I also cannot imagine anyone else, apart from me, who would tolerate your particular quirks of behaviour ... just sayin' ... (smiley emoji) My favourite times are when we are sharing our ideas and passion for our craft – as actors we certainly understand each other! My least favourite conversations concern the small mundanities of life that we always try to be the boss of ... just sayin' ... (laughing emoji)

Your talent continues to be an aphrodisiac, you make me laugh and you live the sort of kindness I aspire to – you have taught me much Mr Coard and for that I'm deeply grateful.

Oh – and the woodpile ... I love the woodpile!

Much love

Me x

Debra Lawrance: best known as Pippa on Home and Away, *Debra has worked successfully in film, television and theatre, and lives in rural bliss with her two sons and* Home and Away *co-star Dennis Coard*

Dear Lover

Thank you …

T: thank you for laughing at all my jokes.

H: holding my hand when I'm lost for words.

A: acting with brilliance, skill and talent.

N: nourishing me daily with delicious meals.

K: knowing me better than I know myself.

Y: yawning only once during one of my shows.

O: organising, nurturing and enriching my life.

U: understanding the love in a winter woodpile.

Much love

Me x

Dennis Coard: born in Belfast, Dennis came to Australia and worked with Telecom until the age of 35 before becoming an actor and a husband to Debra Lawrance

Dear Lover

The first time I saw you, I thought about swallowing my tongue so I'd have an excuse not to talk to someone so beautiful. Not that I didn't want to … just that I didn't feel worthy of your ears, so defined and flappable like a flying baby elephant – but with no trunk and a sparkling smile. You were above me and I knew it. A wombat has no place flirting with the majestic queen of crocodiles … for the wombat's place is a hole in the dirt.

You walked into the bookstore that I was killing time in and immediately I hid the corny rom-com I was reading and picked up something more sophisticated in James Joyce. I had never read his work before but I'd heard chatter of how intellectual his writing was and that was how I wanted you to see me – Beau 'the Brain' Windon.

You wandered down the aisle I was loitering in and slowly the dance began as you reached for a book near me, the stepping back and stepping in, the 'Sorry's and 'It's okay's, the scuffling around so you could better shuffle through the books in front of me until you found what you were looking for.

Your eyes caught mine and King-Kong-punched them to the ground, a smirk sliding across your lips in the way that ramen broth slides down my chin during my chaotic consumption of the exquisite cuisine. We stood, silent, and close – flicking through our respective books with purpose.

I telepathically pleaded with any ghosts that may be watching us for them to give me a sign if you had the same desire in your mind as I did. Words from a page I could not make out danced through your soul and held you, tight yet gently, bringing you to let out a slight giggle. It was that moment when I saw it – our future.

You asking me if I'd like to grab coffee.

Me saying that I'd already had three today and probably shouldn't.

You saying *'What about some juice?'*

Me saying *'Juice would be great, I'm craving some pineapple and watermelon.'*

Us at the juice bar and me wondering if this is you showing interest in me or if you were just being nice.

You asking me where I lived.

Me saying *'Nearby, actually.'*

You saying *'Oh, can you show me that special edition of* Green Lantern's Blackest Night *that you were talking about?'*

Us going back to my place and me wondering if you sitting so close to me was some kind of sign that you were interested in me, or if you were just absent-minded and nonchalant about our bodies touching.

You snuggling up to me because *'It's so cold, warm me.'*

Me standing up abruptly to turn the heater on.

You staring at me strangely.

Me wondering if I had annoyed you by not telling you what I was standing up to do.

You coming up to me and putting your lips on mine.

Us, kissing out-of-nowhere as if we were characters in a corny rom-com that some lonely nitwit would flick through in a bookstore while convincing himself that he is completely fine with being single because he has his creative outlets and that's the real love of his life ... that and the ridiculous artform of professional wrestling.

Me saying *'I'm sorry.'*

You saying *'What for?'*

Me saying *'Kissing you without permission.'*

You saying *'No, I kissed you, dingbat.'*

Me saying *'Oh yeah.'*

And then you took the book you were reading to the counter, you paid for it, and you left.

I put down James Joyce and went back to my corny rom-com and thought to myself that I should write about you in the near-impossible hope that you read it and realise that you were the person I was daydreaming about (in full colour) in the bookstore. But then, I think of how that's a stupid thought so I file you away as a momentary crush in time ... and I go home so I can spend time with the loves of my life, watching wrestling and writing silly little things.

Best of love

Beau the Bleeding Heart Windon

Beau Windon: neurodivergent writer. If you see him in the wild, approach him with caution and offer a choc-orange treat

Dear Lover

I was thinking that you would rescue me and shelter me from the storms in life, but I was so broken and bruised, I couldn't receive love, I couldn't accept it.

So when the bad memories came, you couldn't change that; when the world got tough, you couldn't rescue me.

When the anger showed its ugly head, you couldn't change that.

I tried to pretend to the world that I was okay, successful, needed and loved but deep down I did not believe it at all.

I tried to blame and justify that you all were at fault until …

The day I realised I needed to rescue myself, I did and in doing that I started to love and accept myself, the bad memories faded and the anger turned to forgiveness and I finally found peace.

Now, dear Lover, I am ready when you are.

Shell

Shellie Morris: multi-award-winning singer–songwriter, who sings in seventeen First Nations languages

Dear Lover

Sorry about my knees.

When we first met I had one good one and one half decent one. I'd snapped the dodgy one in two about ten years earlier, playing footy. A pop so loud the other players stood around me in disbelief before calling for the stretcher. The operation to put it back together went fairly well (for the public system anyway), but twenty years of fast in-swing bowling has well and truly worn the shine off that. It's been bone on bone for years. And then I did my good knee recently throwing a fellow thesp across a backyard in a fight scene. At least with two rubbish knees there's no limp anymore. Just a weird crab-like gait that looks like I have a test tube up my clacker I don't want to break. Very attractive.

Remember when we could jump from position to position – doggy to wheelbarrow to reverse cowgirl to golden arch with smooth, acrobatic agility? Now it's tricky just trying to get into missionary without all the hollering and creaking and clicking and moaning (and I don't mean the fun type). At least it doesn't last too long, I guess …

But hey, at our age it's not all about the sexy-stuffs (as we obliquely call it), is it? Thank God. As you said to me one sunny morning years ago – we're a team. Once it was the team of you, me and our pooch. These days it's the team of you, me and our teenager. The team with bad knees but a helluva lot of love.

Slem

Steve Le Marquand: character stage and TV actor who takes cricket and rugby league quite seriously

Dear Lover

I could say about ten billion things. Ten billion words, ten billion quotes, ten billion songs about how much I completely and utterly adore you. Every single insecurity, every single little flaw you have, I love it. I love it all. I love all of you, forever and always.

You are my person, you are my sunlight, you make me smile through salty tears. You make me feel like dancing in the rain, like running into the forest with your hand in mine. You are the blooming spring flowers and the buzz of the bees, you are the frost in the winter and the sparks in the fire. I could hear you talk about anything, just to hear your voice. It makes me feel so alive knowing you are living beside me, and I am not whole without you. The gods must have been in a good mood when they decided to drop you onto the earth, because you are nothing short of divine.

Yes, you have been hurt, and you have flaws. You are imperfect and stubborn, but that is quite honestly why I love you. You don't have to be perfect, not for me, not for anyone. You are simply you, and I admire that beyond anything in this universe. I feel like I have known you long before this lifetime, and I know that I will see you again afterwards. I hope that someday soon your hand will find mine. You'll give me that beautiful, stupid smile. You'll tell me not to cry and you'll hold me again.

But for now, dear Lover, just know that I love you so.

Clem

Charlie Le Marquand: a thirteen year old who is a love enthusiast

Dear Lover

It's funny calling you 'lover'. Of all the terms of endearment I've used for you, my favourite is definitely 'best friend'.

I don't know how I'd be without you beside me. It's a rocky road being a touring musician, and without your help to steer the ship I'd be lost. (I know I've mixed my metaphors there and that'll drive you crazy, but that's all part of my charm.)

When we first met at the *Bella* album launch at the Tamworth Country Music Festival in 2004, you were doing sound and I was in awe of your technical ability. I had no idea who you were and we were on very different paths then, but I do remember smiling at the monitor engineer throughout the entire performance! You got a copy of our CD and played it for years.

Fast forward to eight years later and we meet again on a Beccy Cole tour. You were doing sound and I was determined to be a nun. I'd had enough of relationships and blokes in general, but Beccy could see that despite all that, I liked you. It took some serious nudging from her to even convince me to acknowledge I thought you were a 'bit of alright' and after our first date (which she orchestrated), I was smitten. Your beautiful singing voice and dry humour continues to leave me weak at the knees.

For ten years we have shared our lives and weathered the highs and lows, and good lord there've been some lows, but we're better than ever, stronger together and I will love you every day that ends with night.

Lynnie

Lyn Bowtell: artistic director of the CMAA Academy of Country Music and multi-Golden Guitar-winning songstress who turned four red chairs in Season 6 of The Voice

Dear Lover

I am perfectly confused. In my eternal quest for you, I really am quite curious. I mean, where in this delicious mystery could you be? It has been the most desperate of seasons. So much distance, it would seem, has developed between us. How exactly did we drift apart? It is said, apparently, by sober analytical types, that time and space are constructs of the mind. What? Do I have to read that again? So, in other words, it has been argued that longing is something made up, imagined almost. How strange. How strange to relegate this sweet yearning, this exquisite ache I feel to the condition of mere fantasy. Surely, if this were the case, satisfaction would be available, right here, right now, twenty-four-seven, beyond this ravenous hunger. I mean, why under this almighty sky would we choose anything else but this boundless instant, this dimension of simply being? And yet our unquenchable thirst remains King ... this craving our holy Queen.

A moment, an hour, an era, an age, a procession of incalculable beauty unfolds within the space of every breath. And yet again, this hollow appetite thrives. Here I am, like a ceaseless junkie tolling the very bell of desire, summoning all that 'appears' to be absent, perpetuating this illusion of lack. Perhaps, dear Lover, I must accept that I was born this way, too stubborn to ever really let go. Perhaps, in fact, I will die this way too, married to my seeking without the space to truly accommodate you … ? Who can say? But one thing I can promise, my darling, one thing I can say for sure, is that I will do everything in my power to relish every morsel that you leave for me along the way … every moonlight, every storm, every cuddle and every form …

With love, light and just a tiny hint of mischief

Damian … xx

Damian Walshe Howling: AFI award-winning actor, writer, director, offensively good looking and equally charming

Dear Lover

Out of the random
You posted something
I understood immediately
I was not myself
until you got me ...
We peeled off our skins
and liked each other's
raw bloodied minds
and bodies
and souls
I thought I had sniffed
You out
In many others
I was wrong
Now here you are

John Howard: Logie Award-winning actor who enjoys reading,
astronomy, golf and lawn bowls

Dear Lover

I am thinking of your hidden flesh, which I will sprinkle with salt, after I lay you down and squish you, pressing gently but firmly; your body spreading across a warm mattress I prepared just for you to lay upon. This is the place where I will taste and bite until you are finished. Where I will make a meal of you. You taught me that breakfast is not a time of day, but a decision to introduce daylight back into my mouth. Lover, you are green with envy when I mention peanut butter or honey. Lover, we are arguing again, about the definition of fruit verses vegetable. Lover, I am suddenly on my knees when you fall from the pinnacle of your supermarket stack. Where you bruise, I ache. As if inside both of us, we share the same stony centre; a hard spot we have both grown our softness from, which will eventually outlive our skin. Lover, there is a tattoo of you on my left shin. Once, a stranger in a train carriage took a photograph of it. I wonder if he sent the photo to a friend. Captioned, 'look at this, look how much this person loves' and the recipient replied with a line of avocado emojis. Lover, I'm sorry the emoji shows you severed in half like a broken heart.

Maddie

Maddie Godfrey: writer, educator, editor, Kat Muscat Fellow. Western Australian Youth Award winner for their 'Creative Contributions' to the state. They are not a morning person

Dear Lover

You keep me on track. Not by being my boss but by being my friend.

You impress me every day but make me feel like I impress you too.

How did I find you in the universe?

I love you more than Chinese sausage and I REALLY love Chinese sausage.

Mart xx

Marty Fields: versatile comedian, actor, author, and Melba Conservatorium trained pianist. Resident comedian on Hey, Hey, It's Saturday *and* Blankety Blanks

Dear Lover

Breath

I fear that you will die
one day
we all do
one day

in bed
being rattled by sound
any sound
I wake
am woken
sound-woken
rattled by all sound

the sound of your breath
breathing
is reassurance
but still I am stuck with wake

rattled
by this simple significant rhythmic sound

but

the sound of your breath
breathing
your next and every breath
despite my pin-drop rattleness
is reassurance
in the wake sound-woken awakeness

… breath is the start and the end of it
I should probably resolve this paranoid death-fix …

but in death
is its opposite
you
lover
your life
my life-love

one day when
you
or I
fail morning wake up
I think
hope think
that the abiding force holding us
will hold us still

when we are each

one

or both

breathless

Penelope

Penelope Bartlau: artist, director, writer and self-proclaimed expert in making shit up

Dear Lover

As I took myself out for coffee that day, I didn't know it was all about to change.

I remember the first sight of you strolling through chaotic tables, brandishing a hot beverage in one hand and empty plates in the other.

My heart resembled a bruised potato from a decade of disappointments; I had mused that the wonder of romance for me now was a worn-out cassette waiting to be rewound by a hard-to-find pen.

And yet, your broad smile was like a moment from a classic movie that I wanted to see again and again.

A few months earlier a cab driver in Memphis had asked me, 'Is there someone at home?' 'No,' I had replied awkwardly. 'Don't worry,' he advised in a quasi-profound tone … there would be someone, and there would be a sign.

His mumbo-jumbo advice popped into my head as I realised it was Astro Boy on your T-shirt … he was my childhood hero and a recurring theme song in my ears.

When I eventually asked you out, my favourite coffee shop was at stake ... but I was prepared to take the risk.

Twelve years on you're still the one, we have even made two small humans that look like us. I sometimes wonder what might have happened without that café. Would we still have met? Would our beautiful children walk this earth if I hadn't had a coffee addiction?

The sight of your smile, the touch of your warm skin and the sound of your whisper are divine treasures to me.

I am balanced by your level-headed perspective and capsized by your sensual shape.

I secretly worry I love you too much, but this is the only way I can love you.

A small plastic Astro Boy sits on my desk, he is winking at me ... I wink back sometimes and we share a knowing smile.

Jimi

Jimi 'the Human' Hocking: rocked out hard with The Angels and The Screaming Jets before moving happily to the blues

Dear Lover

Please make yourself known.

Sooz Camilleri

Sue Camilleri: much loved Love Your Sister villager, national music PA and publicist

Dear Lover

That's you, Wayne. Lover of 24 years.

This is an apology. I am so truly sorry for fainting when you had your vasectomy.

You were the one who had endured the day surgery, yet I was the one in the recovery chair whom the nurses refused to release.

It was so embarrassing. It's not as if I watched the operation; unlike childbirth, there isn't a guest list for vasectomies and partners are not asked to cheer from the sidelines. One minute I was standing next to you sitting up on the bed, and the next minute I was lying on the cold tiles, blocking the entrance to the toilet. I know this because a man with a thick Russian accent was yelling for someone to move me because he needed to give a stool sample.

The thing is, the procedure had gone well. You were a little groggy when I came to pick you up but you were recuperating nicely. I had absolutely no reason to be alarmed, and yet I passed out.

In the weeks that followed I began to see that our decision not to have any more children had hit me hard. I had been grappling with our inevitable mortality and when I understood that I was contemplating vast and fundamental ideas about life and death, I realised why I had fainted.

So why then did I also faint when you had a splinter in your foot?

Admittedly, it was actually a ten-centimetre shard of wood but, still, the moment was not about me, and I'm very sorry that I ended up on the floor of the emergency department as you were carted off to a ward.

You and I both know 'faint' is my fancy word for 'panic attack'. The thought of anything bad happening to you makes my body try to shut my brain down: nothing to see here, folks. I've been so cross with my shonky wiring over the years but, lately, I've come to admire my default setting. Because, actually, it's impossibly romantic.

In nineteenth-century literature, someone's always conking out. They're forever waving smelling salts after someone's swooned. That's what I'm doing. Not fainting, swooning. That's why it's in all the classics. Is there a greater declaration of love than the total surrender of your central nervous system?

So, I am very sorry, but I cannot promise that you won't continue to make me swoon, over and over again.

Love

Robyn

*Robyn Butler: actor, writer, director, producer, prolific content creator (*The Librarians, Upper Middle Bogan, Summer Love*) and married to Wayne Hope*

Dear Lover

I actually find it hard to call you that because the song 'Lover, Lover, Lover' pops into my head and the next line is about not being treated well and that's just not true – you treat me with love and respect and you always give me your undivided attention. I wish I could say I give you the same attention all the time, but I can't, not since the night you gave birth to our daughter, Emily, twenty years ago.

We were living in that old weatherboard rental in Elsternwick, which I hated. The back half of the house had sunk so badly that I swore we'd gather speed as we went down the hallway. We really had to make an effort to pull ourselves up at the kitchen or we'd go straight out the back door. I moaned about it a lot, I think I was pretty anxious all round. How were we supposed to nest in such a shitty nest? You didn't seem to care as much, I think because you were focused on the fact you were giving birth imminently. You knew what was coming, you'd already had beautiful Molly, my stepdaughter, seven years earlier. Focus on the breath, fuck the floorboards.

When the contractions started it really threw me, despite having nine months prep time, because I didn't know what to-do and you know I like to-do things. Lots of things. You've rightly pointed out that I get a chunk of my self-worth from ticking things off a never-ending to-do list – that I create. I've given it a name: SOMHWC (son of migrants hamster wheel complex).

But from the first contraction, it was clear you had rightly taken command of the to-do list and would work away on it for the next 26 hours. Unable to act on my action imperative, I pathetically followed you around the house and nodded at you with a stupid facial expression that tried to convey 'I understand honey, I get it and I'm here'. I was useless until about the fifteen-hour mark when, in the lounge room, you asked if you could lean on me, literally. Sitting was no longer bearable for you and you were tired of pacing and you said the best position for you was to stand up and put your arms around my neck and drop your head and be still. So you did that – for the next three hours.

It was kind of something to-do?

At around the two-hour mark, I became aware of the TV on behind me. It was the FIFA World Cup, being played in Korea and Japan. As you know, I don't respond to sport – with one exception: the World Cup. I say it's because I only have to focus on sport for a couple of weeks every few years and then I can converse with most Australian men, but really it's because the World Cup is one of the few fond memories I have with my father. When I was four or five years old he would get me up in the middle of the night to watch the Netherlands play. 'Go oranje' (orange), he would yell at our black and white telly. It was confusing but I loved that he was happy – that was pretty rare. He wasn't a great dad. Anyway, as you were steadily planted, gripping me, in hour three, I heard Germany and Saudi Arabia had started to play. Right out of the gates, Germany scored, and then they scored again, and then another. 3–0 within minutes. I remember the commentator saying 'I think you might be watching something special right now'.

Problem was, I wasn't hon, I was watching the top of your head and a cracked plaster wall.

Now, Dr Freud might say it was pretty bloody obvious that the thoughts of my own disappointing father and the fact that I was about to become one myself were overwhelming and it was, in fact, a happy accident that I was being forced to remember something good about my dad. But I hadn't joined the dots yet. I just needed to watch that game. I started to gently reposition us and turn you around. I did it slowly, imperceptibly. It was a gentle rock from side to side. It took me four more goals to spin you right around but I did it, I finally faced the TV at the 90-minute mark as Germany scored its historic eighth goal. We both screamed, for different reasons.

Clearly I've carried this for a long time and I want to confess it to you. I'm sorry for not giving you my undivided attention that night, like you have so often done for me in times of crisis.

Actually, there's only one time I can remember you not really being physically there with me. Remember when I got my vasectomy?

Love you

Wayne

Wayne Hope: actor, writer, director and producer at Gristmill, the acclaimed production company he founded with his wife, Robyn Butler

Dear Lover

I dreamt of you twice last night, which is not unusual. The first was predictable – me searching for you again in a crowded street in some ancient city, catching a glimpse of the back of your head at a market stall and calling out, but of course you not hearing me then disappearing before I can reach you. I was plotting my next move when the 4 a.m. Norwegian sun snaked through the gaps in the blinds and woke me – and so I stopped dreaming and began to think.

Remember that airport queue in Chicago? You stood across in Boarding Group A, wearing black jeans, a soft green jumper and with your hair pulled back into a tight ponytail. I took a photo, expecting to capture your proud, elegant profile as you stared straight ahead, dignified but impatient. Instead, at the last moment, you turned to me and scowled – and though that scowl twisted itself into a smirk, the image captured was one of menace. That photo was lost with the phone that took it, but it remains my favourite – printed, framed and hung in my mind, ready to haunt me at 4.05 a.m. in some sterile hotel room when I'm so far away from you.

I slept again, and this time in my dream we lay, your head resting on my chest, the way we did so long ago, before anything happened, when our love was a complicated friendship, fuelled by desire and chastened by responsibility. I kissed you on the forehead and, content, let myself drift towards dreamless sleep. The kind that might nourish me just enough to face another day, without you.

Whilst remaining always yours

Lachlan

Lachlan Bryan: morally ambiguous but generally kind alt-country musician (The Wildes)

Dear Lover

If I could stretch the meaning of the word and include you, our two days and nights in Venice, I don't think you would mind. For we both know the biological function of fantasy, of the idea of us being bigger than the apartment we shared.

I feel I should just enjoy those moments, whether only romantic because of place and circumstance. The excitement of taking in so much art so close, the splendour of the city, being by water, our bodies.

I cried in the Turkish Pavilion, feeling free for the first time in so long, like I could tear away from the constant anxiety. Here was something to live for.

Your face that evening as you sampled figs with goat's cheese. You seemed to savour the end. When we got back to the apartment, I was quick to shut my bedroom door. For the risk outweighed the reward.

The next morning we moved early. Found coffee and croissants at the cutest place available. I had shopping on my mind. You followed me into a place with local designs. Alerted me to an indigo boilersuit you insisted was made for me. You gasped sincerely when I emerged from the fitting room. The mirror confirmed, I did look cool. My gender affirmation senses were tingling. There was a person underneath all that fear. I picked out a showstopper piece for you, per your request. Gold accentuates your neck.

You are beautiful when you run along the canal. There's a point to proximity.

I did not tell you this directly. You are going home, to Lenapehoking, and me, Turrbal. Venice was shared between us and we indulged in a closeness I won't forget.

Love

EvN x

Ellen van Neerven: award-winning author, editor and educator of Mununjali (Yugambeh language group) and Dutch heritage

Dear Lover

I remember we met on stage performing together in *West Side Story*. When I saw you my heart skipped a beat, Tony and Maria's romance was not the only one singing, there was also you and me.

You thought I would only be good for the twelve-month tour, but here we are 38 years later, one child, a mortgage, and still travelling down life's road together.

We are so compatible now that when we get intimate, we even get a headache at the same time.

Love

Wayne

Wayne Scott Kermond: fourth generation award-winning song and dance man

Dear Lover

I apologise. For the times I confused you with Love. For your names are very similar and, for a long time, I was too young to know the difference, too willing to believe you were one and the same. I didn't know that such high expectations would only make you doomed to fail.

You were not Love, you were just a lover. Planted in my life to show me how to better love myself.

With gratitude

Matilda

Matilda Brown: writer, director, actor and passionate regenerative farming advocate

Dear Lover

When you were here, you were gone. Now that you're gone,
you are here.

Forgetting me. Loving me. Forgetting loving me.

I look for you and I can't find you. When I don't look for
you, there you are.

Always hiding, always seeking, always penetrating my mind.

Heart. I penetrated your heart then squashed it. You pierced
my soul and took it with you.

I look forward but see what is behind me. You look back but
see the future.

A future bright. Love. Ongoing beauty. Me in my abandoned
retrospect.

Asunder the tenderness, the play, the life. Together in our
souvenirs of the past.

But life, but life, life. It is what I crave. Look, here. I love so
much. Love all.

My nurturers – the life people, my friends. What would I do?
A life without would be too frightening.

Soul. Sky, water, current. Love. Current love. Yes hard, and
good. Good.

Real and imaginable. True. A kind veracity. Kind – kinder in
the garden.

My gardener, so grateful am I. You seeded me and I needed
you. Grow.

Growing love that may sweep the ocean around us and
through us and between us and under us and over us and
not tear away. Tear.

No more, the weeping. That is sleeping.

I awake and love. Heart. Penetrate me. Bright.

Lover dear.

George Ellis

*George Ellis: conductor, composer and musical arranger who has
made a stellar career of combining symphony orchestras with popular
artists*

Dear Lover

I miss you when you leave the room.
I love you.
Thank you for everything that you are.

Ben Gillies: member of legendary Australian band Silverchair, winner of 21 ARIA awards and one of the world's most respected drummers

Dear Lover

I never met you because I hadn't met the man we have in common when you died. He is my lover now, but he was yours when you died.

In the first year of he and I's relationship I went to see a clairvoyant wanting to know more about you.

'I'm not sure if this is within the realm of what you can do.'

'You want me to speak to a dead person? I *can* do it, but I don't *like* to do it.'

She could see you wearing a miniskirt and tall boots. Not that you literally wore those, but that outfit represented hedonism. She felt you had been flirting with youth being with him. Mucking around dating a bartender so many years younger than yourself. You weren't going to end up together. She saw that, had you lived, you would've settled down with someone who wore a suit.

I don't believe that clairvoyants can speak to the dead or predict the future. I believe they make us feel better about the present.

He quit the bar after you died. That was years ago. He has shorter hair now. It's begun to bald since we've been together. He got promoted recently. He wears a suit to work.

He is yours as much as he is mine.

Allee

Allee Richards: lighting technician and author of the illuminating Small Joys of Real Life

Dear Lover

… Lizzy :)

It's strange
How when I try to think of a word
Or a sentence
That could possibly encapsulate my love
Gratitude
And the depth of what you mean to me …

My mind empties

Upon further reflection
I guess it IS that all encompassing silence
And the deep contentment found within it

That best expresses
What I truly wish to say.

Love

Luke

Luke O'Shea: multi-awarded singer–songwriter whose voice is said to be found somewhere between Midnight Oil and John Williamson

Dear Lover

There is a scene in the English version of *The Office* where David Brent mentions 'Taffy' who works in the warehouse. Well, before I'd watched it with subtitles I thought it was 'Tuffy' and for some reason the way he said it really made me laugh so that's how he got his name. I was watching *The Office* a lot when we were living in the mountains ... turns out mountains don't suit me, they make me feel like I'm suffocating. I'd been out of work for ages and the isolation was wearing me down. The days were long and boring and I was struggling to snap out of my funk so you thought I should meet him and maybe it would cheer me up.

The day we met is still so clear in my mind, the sun was blazing hot and we drove down a dusty, isolated road to his house. When I got there it was chaos, with his brothers jumping all over me and I could see him at the back being pushed out of the way. He was so desperate to say hello but too nervous to take his place at the front, and when I looked into his big brown eyes I knew we were meant to be. You knew instantly that he was my son and you were right because we were inseparable from the start. I talked about him incessantly, actually it started getting a little weird and my family had to have a mini intervention, but I was crazy in love and I couldn't help myself.

He could be annoying sometimes though, like humping all of our visitors or when I would pack to go away he would pee in my suitcase in the hope of stopping me leaving. He also thought he could fly ... that was pretty stressful. That time he rolled in an old dead wombat wasn't stellar either, and I called you to come and save us because he was covered in guts and maggots and I was panicking. Maggots are a deal-breaker. He liked to steal dirty nappies too, which was revolting – especially when he would dive in face first. However, these were minor indiscretions because for the most part he was perfect.

He was anxious a lot and storms freaked him out but I didn't mind his anxiety, I felt like I could make sense of it. In fact, I feel like I understood him completely. When the kids came into his life do you remember how his personality changed instantly? He went from the crazy speedster that zipped around incessantly to the protector with the job of a lifetime. Every picture I have with the kids, there he was ... always. Do you think he felt like he was second fiddle when they were babies? I hope not because he was the one who got me out of the house every day and into the fresh air, saving me again. I mean it was hard to juggle a pram, a toddler and Tuffy, but I did it. I think I did okay. I swore a lot ... I feel bad about that.

I'm not sure when it changed, I guess I was so distracted by my own ageing process that I failed to notice his. One day I realised that his eyes were cloudy and instead of playing with me he just wanted to sleep on me. We did alright in those years, didn't we? 'Sixteen years is a good innings' people would say, but it didn't help … it just made it harder. When he didn't want to walk anymore I took him everywhere in my arms so he could see the world, because he was my extra limb and I didn't know if I could stay upright without him. I started making gags calling him 'Weekend at Bernie's' because I was carrying him around trying to keep him alive when I knew he didn't want to be. I'm sorry I dragged it out for so long, but I didn't know how to let him go.

You knew it was time but I wasn't ready, and so we walked around with a pain in our hearts. Sometimes I hid how bad it was because I could tell you knew it was over and I was scared you would rush me. You didn't though, you waited for me to get there and when I did you looked after me. When we pulled up outside the little white building for his final visit you took your foot off the brake, looked at me and said, 'One more lap'. I realised then that he wasn't just my everything but he was everything to both of us. So we did one more lap of the block before we said goodbye.

'Never again,' I said and I lay in bed for a week feeling like I couldn't breathe … I never wanted to feel that pain again. I was resolved, he was my first and he would be my last. My one and only. I was so broken and sad and I was struggling to snap out of my funk so you thought I should meet someone to cheer me up. Once I looked into those big brown eyes I wondered if maybe I wasn't broken after all. Maybe this story wasn't over.

There is a great scene that the kids love in *Gremlins* where Randall meets the Mogwai in the thrift store and names him Gizmo ... so that's how he got his name.

Dear Lover, thank you.

Pia

Pia Miranda: Australian entertainment industry sweetheart

Dear Lover

I know I'm bad at it.

I'm aware this frustrates you.

Your previous paramours have executed it with such *finesse*.

I'm too impatient to perfect it.

This Valentine's Day, however, I'm gonna nail it.

My gift to you is … learning to stack the dishwasher.

To date, my approach is like a magic trick gone wrong. I haphazardly hurl those dirty dishes into the air and – *Huzzah!* – hope some wizardry will sort out the rest. Alas, not much alchemy going on in the old Whirlpool. Cutlery assembled like a drunken army in disorderly rows. Baking dishes lying supine, still clinging to last night's lasagne. Cups runneth over with grey, greasy water. The spray arms thwacking the upright jar providing the deafening *doof doof* of a deep thumping bass.

But this will all change, dear Lover. I've done some stack swotting. There's a *science* to loading dishes. Engineers at the University of Birmingham tracked water movements in dishwashers. Not sure how that little engineer guy survived a full cycle but anyway, those boffins discovered The Definitive Way To Load Dishes.

First, don't overload. Second, pack dishes with protein on them, like egg, closer to the edge at lower heights allowing the detergent to work. Third, mount carb-stained/caked-on-tatties-type dishes near the centre or the top shelf where they receive the water jets' full force. Finally, if you want to get fancy, stack plates in a circular pattern.

Who needs Barry White when you have the gentle hum of a correctly stacked dishwasher to get you in the mood.

Love

Elise

Elise Elliott: journalist, radio presenter, writer, podcast host and rev-head

Dear Lover

Where do I start with writing this to the most amazing human in my life!?

I thought about writing this in a funny way and having a laugh, however, I feel like that's what our whole relationship is, as we really are best mates.

So here goes what I really think of you, the angel in my life.

I'm so grateful we have found each other. I'm so very blessed to have you as the mother of our beautiful daughter; my greatest achievement to date so far is that beautiful little girl!

You're the best mother to her already and I know you always will be. You have a tough gig looking after a baby girl and a 32-year-old man–child in me, haha, but you do it with ease.

We have gone through so much together and you've never even looked like leaving my side. You're amazing.

I often joke you're such a lucky lady to have me, but I'll be honest here, it's definitely me who's the lucky one!

Thanks so much for having my back in the darkest of times and thanks so much for laughing and smiling with me in the best times.

I love so much about you: I love your morals, I love how beautiful your soul is, I love your smile (it really could light up a dark room), I love your laugh, I love how loyal you are to the ones you love, the list really goes on. I just love you!

Alright that's enough soppy words to you from me now, Knackers. Back to being best mates it is.

I have a tough guy rep to keep, haha.

Love ya

Jase xx

Jason Whateley: pugilist, new dad and the current Australian Cruiser Weight Champion

Dear Lover

We were just two kids when we started dating, and in that special moment when you stared deeply into my eyes at our favourite restaurant in Geelong, I knew I had found the love of my life.

You have stood by me through the best and the worst times in my life and you also raised our two babies at home while I was constantly touring. You have always put yourself last and never once complained. I love the way you love our kids unconditionally, and I am so proud of you for kicking so many goals with your own career. You really are an amazing wife and mother.

You are a beautiful, confident, strong, patient woman and I love your sense of humour. (Especially the time when I opened my suitcase in America only to find that you had replaced all of my undies with yours! It still makes me laugh.) You are my rock and the heart and soul of our family. Although we don't show you enough, the kids and I would be lost without you.

Dear Lover, you are my soul mate and I am so grateful that you chose me to share your life with.

I will love you forever and ever amen!

Adam

Adam Harvey: country music star and keeper of so many Golden Guitars that he's started selling them on eBay

Dear Lover

By which I mean, dear lovers. Plural.

Dear beloveds.
Dear sweethearts.
Dear partners.
Yes, there's more than one of you.
But you already know that.

You know each other as friends, as companions, as also-partners. (If my partner's partner is also my partner, is that partner to the power of two? Partner^2?)

But I digress.
Dear lovers,

At school I didn't understand the need for monogamy or the fuel of jealousy. Companionship, community and collaboration was what I wanted in life but assumed no one could offer.

Then I read the word polyamory (the practice of having multiple partners, with the informed consent of each other).

Then I met each of you.

And everything blossomed into the beautiful relationships I cherish today: our pasta dinners and pub nights, our sleepy bedtime cuddles, our little slice of multi-partnered paradise.

Of course, it wasn't always this simple. There were years of soul-searching and anguish and wondering why I couldn't just be 'normal'.

But 'normal' is such a myth, isn't it? No one person's relationship looks the same as another. We all craft our own 'normal' – our lives are our own to explore and embrace.

And this life? I want it forever. I want to hold your hands and then curse not having enough hands for all the love I've been given.

I want to be the very best version of myself with each of you by my side.

Dear lovers,

Dear partners,

Dear loves of my life,

Thank you for taking a chance on this tattooed, book-loving, weird little poet.

Thank you for being the best versions of yourself as we walk beside each other, hand-in-hand-in-hand-in-hand, exploring this world together.

Rae White: award-winning non-binary transgender poet, writer, educator and zine maker

Dear Lover

I'm not sure I will ever have another lover like you ... we had one perfect summer that is still carved into my very being and soul.

A knock at the door ... I open it ... you standing there with nothing but red lace Agent Provocateur lingerie ... covered only by your long black overcoat and black leather thigh-high boots. Not a word said between us ... like magnets, our mouths are drawn together as we make our way to the kitchen bench ... knocking over anything and everything that gets in our way. Like magic, our clothes disappear and we are instantly transported to my bedroom, completely naked, wrapped in each other's warm sensual embrace ... the smell of you lightly shaded by the scent of your jasmine perfume.

The way you used to run your long nails down my back ... the softness of your skin ... the expressions on your face ... the kisses we shared as if our mouths were made for each other – a perfect connection when our tongues would touch. The feeling of climax that lasted forever ... but never quite long enough ...

I loved how we started our nights together way back then, when we were young and nothing mattered but the moment and being in the moment. Not until we were in a post-coital state did we come up for air and words came from our mouths.

A long-lasting memory ... you lying in my bed with the sheets half wrapped around your curves ... champagne ... fresh berries ... the perfect masterpiece still etched in my mind ... still so vivid in my memory after all these years.

Love

A⏐ xxx

Alex Lloyd: multi-platform ARIA-winning musician

Dear Lover

We've never celebrated Valentine's Day. You shouldn't need an excuse to express true love, we've always said.

So, I admit it's a little weird that I'm writing to you in a book of love letters. Add to that the fact I was once a card-carrying member of MAPDA (Men Against Public Displays of Affection) and it's even stranger I'm doing this.

But, our love has always been an exception.

A love that survived cancer against the odds of death or divorce. A love that created two amazing children, despite us being told we should never have kids. A love that has seen me let you put your leg over my stomach in bed, even if said leg is hotter than liquid magma.

The thing is, *you're* exceptional. You're kinder than anyone I've met. You prove impossible things are possible, just because someone said you couldn't do it. You inspire me daily with your passion and compassion. That's why I love you and always will.

Tara. Boombadarts. Wasabi Duck Face. Let's continue to be an exception. Let's stay together till we're ghosts.

Love

Timmy

Tim Hawken: award-winning author of If Kisses Cured Cancer

Dear Lover

I'm not actually sure you exist. I guess that's okay if you don't. I like my own company. It's taken me a while to work out who I am and learn to love the person I've become. Perhaps you've been on the same journey? I believe for a relationship to work, we can't be that person's 'other half'. We both need to be complete people. And I am a complete person. A particularly weird person, but still complete. You aren't 'normal' are you? I'm not really sure how to handle 'normal' people.

There is a quote that says, 'Stop waiting for your Prince Charming. Get up and find him. The poor idiot may be stuck in a tree or something.' Well, I've climbed plenty of trees, but haven't found you yet. If you are out looking for me, I could still be up a tree (or hanging off an aerial circus apparatus), or more likely just at home chilling with my cats – as a single woman in my 30s, I have already accepted my feline allocation from the adoption agency.

So that's where I'll be, pretending to be working on my next novel and being impressed that my houseplants are still alive. (Turns out the trick is to build them all out of Lego.)

Whoever you are, wherever you are, I hope you are happy and maybe we will run into each other some day.

Nikki

PS I don't do Valentine's Day. It's an overrated, commercialised day to make people think they have to spend money to show affection. So I hope you bought this book because the proceeds go to charity and not as a gift to your current girlfriend, because that would be really awkward.

Nikki Moyes: author of young adult and speculative fiction who lives with her cats

Dear Lover

This letter is to you. This letter is not to coffee, which is full bodied and invigorating; the black gold that starts life every day. That's not love. This letter isn't to the films of Paul Verhoeven, which are so good and are even better than James Cameron's – a minority opinion. This letter is not to the Boston Celtics or to the music of Robyn, or to when someone comes and brings cold beers to Tamarama Beach, where we've been playing volleyball for hours, at sunset. This letter is not to the third day after finishing a book, when some modicum of relief and pride is allowed in. This letter is not to any of these, even though before you they all would warrant a letter of love. Not now. My love letters are only for you now. Love is not ironic for me now, nor hyperbolic. Love is love now, real and simple. It's a stake in the ground never to be removed. It's a flag on my uniform. This love letter is to you, Claire, and it needs to say only this: I love you.

Ben

Ben Mckelvey: bestselling author who turned a heart attack in his twenties into an inspiring, no-fear, globetrotting career

Dear Lover

I was grieving and angry when your kind words woke me. I was determined not to let loss define me. I had decided to choose love and light but still, every day was a battle. You spoke into my pain and made me feel understood and cared for. You didn't really know me then, but somehow you did. The words you chose were the very ones I needed and they came right on time.

When I was feeling rejected and worthless you respected and valued me. You didn't just hear my despair, you listened to it. You didn't try to make my pain disappear, you walked beside me in it, giving me the space to take the steps I needed for myself. You became my lover – the one I love. Sweet words and warm feelings are lovely but I believe the act of giving of yourself is what love truly is. When we do that for each other, every need we have is more than met. I love how comfortably we sit in that space. I love you.

The years have taught me that much of life is outside of my control and things can change in a flash. In an instant I was left stranded, holding onto words that may have made a difference but now can never be heard. It's important that the people you love deeply know it, and I'm writing this to you so that you'll always have a reminder that I love you, no matter what.

Hiss xx

Felicity Urquhart: multi-award-winning songstress

Dear Lover

You will arrive on my doorstep, shining in the moonlight, free of baggage. I will still be buckling under the weight of my own. You will have arms of steel but a soft palm, holding out a magnolia seed that you would like to plant. I will traipse into the garden and drop it into a plastic pot, to show you that I do sometimes exercise.

You will see all the housework to be done, and you will miraculously do it. I will loll around on the couch as you prepare to vacuum, explaining why I refuse to perpetuate the gendered division of domestic labour. You will ask me thoughtful questions about myself. I will be surprised to be fielding any. You will be funny. I will suggest that I am funnier.

You will be a calm operator. I will have a mind that runs dark and wild. You will sit close by and wait for the bad weather to pass. I will drift far but always return.

You will take no issue with how I look. I will never, in your view, be asking for it. You will not gaslight me, betray me, humiliate me, discard me, then lie to the world that I have been lucky to have you. I will be comforted, knowing that I will never again feel desperately alone in the company of a man.

You will grow old and collapse one day, after walking me into the garden. We'll have been admiring the first pink bud on our little magnolia tree. I will sob into your shoulder blades and fumble for the key between them, trying to wind you back up.

Julie

Julie Koh: award-winning author and emerging hermit

Dear Lover

It's been a fair few years since we've played Rancid's *And Out Come the Wolves* album, probably our wedding, I reckon, fifteen years back and a decade into our relationship but it's still in the record collection, hey, and always will be, because of course it's important, canon for us really, just bedrock, given that Rancid was cranking out 'Junkie Man' at that festival when I first saw you across a crowded mosh pit and loved you then without space or time for any other from that goddamn moment and although it took you a bit longer, a buzz cut and a bar job, when you stayed the night in Collingwood you never left and still haven't and I remember the song playing in that retro clothes shop in Tokyo and how we yammered at the owner about Rancid and how we met and how we married and I don't think he understood, while our child, high on Pokémon cards and the lights of Akihabara, cruised the shelves in search of treasure, I think I bought a hat but don't quote me because that's not the memory, the memory is you and me and child and Rancid and Tokyo and permanence, and our child is fifteen now and glorious, several people have died since and we have cried and felt the scabrous cost of time passing and libido fading and wearing glasses just to read but we're still here and still in love and laughing every day and Rancid is a fucking great band, hey?

Andrew

Andrew Masterson: king of science and master of crime fiction. Andrew is a devoted author and journalist with high-end credits, who loves his family, chickens and Guinness

Dear Lover

When we met, I thought I knew love. I still believed, I think, in soul mates. The right person, waiting for me.

You taught me something quite unexpected. You taught me that the concept of a soul mate is ridiculous, and worse than that, lazy. It suggests that love is found, like a dropped five dollar note on the street; that once you locate the perfect other half to yourself, that you will finally be complete and happy from that day forward, forever.

You taught me that humans are already whole, and that the work of love isn't in the finding, it's in the making. Love isn't found. It's built.

If you stop believing in soul mates and accept that there are, statistically, at least thousands of humans with whom you could probably have a pretty good relationship, then the idea of picking one person and saying: 'You. Of all the billions of humans on this earth, it is you I want to build a life with,' then that becomes a statement of extraordinary, truly romantic bravery.

And importantly, love becomes a shifting thing, a house that is always being renovated. It becomes a process of learning, of changing, of surprise and of recognition. Love becomes a way of understanding another person, while they come to understand you. That understanding deepens. It broadens. It does not cease. Love is a grand journey undertaken together. And like all truly meaningful work, even when it's hard, it is satisfying and joyous.

Lover, with you, the work is always good. Together, we're building something, teaching each other how to be right for one another. Thank you for showing me that love shouldn't be a thing you find, but rather, a thing you do.

With love

Sarah

Sarah Walker: awarded creative non-fiction writer, artist and photographer

Dear Lover

What can I say, it has been one hell of a journey. We have both changed so much over the last 27 years. You started as a ... how can I say this without offence ... A bit of a wanker, from smashing glasses in a hand and wearing sunglasses on a plane to nearly ruining my publicity career by insulting Alicia Silverstone at a dinner, but there was always something that made me look past all that huff and puff. It may have been our first kiss after four dates, which really did make the world spin. To this day 27 years later I still think of that kiss, which felt like it was the connection of two souls.

Our first date, we knew we were meant to be. The flutter in the stomach, the giddiness that you get when you truly and finally discover what love is. It must have been love as within six weeks you were living with me and my son in a tiny house in the back of someone else's yard in Ringwood North. Within three months we were engaged. Six months later we were married and starting our adventure. I still remember twelve months after meeting you when I sat on your lap to tell you that we were having a child together, your reaction was not quite what I expected. The next ten words that came out of your mouth were simply *Fuck, Fuck* ... once finally you could take a breath from your fucks, your next words were 'I am not worthy to create life', which is probably true but our son was on his way whether you were worthy or not.

Those early days are a blur with three little kids at home and starting our business, but I always felt supported and loved. Let's not kid ourselves, we have had our moments and I have at times called you the worst names I could possibly think of, and it was always deserved. (Well, I thought so anyways.)

I love that you support me in whatever crazy plan I have, from the time when I was 39 and told you I wanted another child and the vasectomy that I made you get after the birth of our third son needed to be reversed; with only a little resistance you went in for the operation. That was unsuccessful so with no complaint you went to get a large needle inserted into your testicles to extract sperm, which eventually resulted in the birth of our beautiful daughter Tahlia.

I sit and look at the incredible family that we have created together, with all their different personalities and the journeys that they are all on, and I think we have done our job. Was bumpy along the way, but with all the things we got wrong and right, they have turned out pretty good.

We are on this great adventure together and I am loving every minute of it. I love that we can be honest and say without offence that we need some time apart, only when we are apart, we miss each other desperately and cannot wait to be in each other's arms again.

I adore and admire the strong, driven and kind man that you are. I feel so lucky that I found 'the one' in this lifetime and I cannot wait to find out what the future holds for us.

My love, my light, I love you with every ounce of my being. You are everything to me.

Your lover

PS You need to sing me that song you wrote.

Janine Allis: founder of Boost Juice Bars, mentor on Shark Tank, *businesswoman and entrepreneur*

Dear Lover

Like so many others, I had been fooled by the story told to us all – the myth colluded upon by fairytales and Hollywood films alike – that love's expression can be only in the most bold and grandiose romantic gestures.

I am still sure that passionate romantic overtures have their place – and I have gratefully received more than my fair share of them. But I want to thank you, dear Lover, for teaching me how love lives not only in the magnificent and extravagant, but equally in the small and the quotidian, the humble and the quiet, the gentle hum of things seemingly everyday, mediocre and even (shock horror, dare I say it) utilitarian and practical.

While our first kiss was a blazing spark of romance under the glow of a bedazzling night sky – quite literally, Vincent van Gogh's *Starry Night* – we also bonded over extolling the virtues of a simple cup of tea. You told me, in hushed reverent tones, 'Sometimes I think love is as simple as putting the kettle on.'

You showed me love can be embodied in sitting on a bench, holding hands, watching the wind ripple through the tree leaves. That it is in acts of care, as much as in grand declarations. When you were sick and I dropped off groceries and food, you messaged me: 'Love is in the soup.'

Don't get me wrong – I love romantic songs, bouquets of flowers, the holding hands while strolling through the evening lights. I adore those stereotypically sweet and commonly socially understood signifiers of love. But I also love how you show me, every day, the way that each small piece of care and each stitch of time can become a patchwork quilt of love that wraps around us.

Louis Armstrong sang that friends saying 'how do you do' are actually saying 'I love you'. My life with you – and with other lovers, and with friends, and with so many people we cross paths with in life – has shown me that this is infinitely true.

'Let me know when you get home safe.'

'I love you.'

'Remember to bring an umbrella!'

'I love you.'

'I saw this interesting rock and thought of you and wanted to show it to you, so I brought it with me – would you like to see it?'

'I love you.'

'I'll put the kettle on just before you get here.'

'I love you.'

Mama

Mama Alto: fierce, femme and fabulous jazz singer, cabaret artiste and gender transcendent diva

Dear Lover

It's kinda pretty magnificent isn't it? I mean, this morning I was playing a Dave Alvin album of songs by Californians about the Golden State and we both started singing along to his version of 'Loser' by Jerry Garcia and Robert Hunter. Not many couples do that.

I'm just happy to have a partner who knows all about Garcia and Hunter and the Grateful Dead … and doesn't get all weirded out that we have (multiple packs of) Grateful Dead playing cards and a Grateful Dead Monopoly game and miniature Grateful Dead tie-dye painted cars and for my 66th birthday knew that what I really wanted was *that* massive 300+ page hardback book about the world of people who recorded thousands of Grateful Dead concerts on cassette. And I love the fact that you hung out with some of those Deadheads and tapers when you first went to America when you were around eighteen years old. And we can share the remorse of never having seen the Dead in concert.

But I digress because tangential conversation is in fact what we do all the time. We can and do on a regular basis start off talking about arcane Grateful Dead trivia and minutes later are holding our sides laughing about a meme that goes 'It was the best of shires ... it was the Worcestershires.' I mean, we KNOW that's hysterically funny, right?

Then we're both ... hold that thought ... in fact I struggle to think of too many things that we disagree over EXCEPT for what may be the biggest one of all. And this, in a strange way, explains why I adore you so much – I can actually deal with sharing my life with a ******* Collingwood supporter. Yes, we both love AFL footy and don't really understand the other games they call football and I know you cheer for the Swans when we go to the games together – which is pretty much always – and manage to contain yourself when it's a Swans/Pies game – but my love for you is such that I DEAL-WITH-IT.

So my life is shared with a Grateful Dead and Collingwood-loving partner – plus a million other things that make our life together so constantly intriguing and invigorating. I reckon that makes me a pretty lucky guy – and – GO SWANS.

Stuart

Stuart Coupe: author, journalist, broadcaster, music commentator

Dear Lover

When I think of '*queer*' – the word and its attachments – I can tell you, honestly, that my overwhelming experience of being queer has been that of yearning.

Rebecca Solnit has an essay in her book *A Field Guide to Getting Lost* where she tells us about Yves Klein's blue monochromes. She writes of blue as something distant, unattainable, and yearned for. And that though you might be able to reach out and touch the skin of the blue monochrome, it remains untouchable because the blue is forever about something *beyond*.

This, I could say, is how it has felt to love *you* all.

First there is *you*, who I meet when I am a teenager in a psych ward. We are sharing a room. When you undress, I see you are wearing men's underwear and that you bind your chest. For reasons I don't understand but feel, I want to know all of you. Your hair is dyed acid blue, and in the quiet of our hospital room, I feel the blue ache of a desire I have no language for.

For several years, I will conflate this deep and untold yearning with being *sick*. I'm in a psych ward, after all …

Then there is *you,* who I meet at a house party in my early twenties. Your hair is dyed the colour of Mars, and between clouds of pink smoke we kiss on a bench top in the dark of the kitchen.

I enter my first threesome this night with you and a guy you have a crush on and feel myself entirely undone. I've fucked so many men by this point, but now I feel myself standing on the wet shore of my new beginning, looking out into open ocean, wind chopped and wild, thinking, *Oh, this was what I have wanted all along. Here I am! I understand it now.*

You don't pursue me. It's him you want. And though I feel again the blue ache of unmet desire, it's the sweetest joy to realise who I am through loving you. Because you give me a word that gives shape to this yearning. I wasn't sick, I realise. I was queer.

Then there is *you,* who I meet when I'm studying at Oxford. We travel during our university holidays to your family's house in the French countryside. It's all wildflowers blooming and skin sparkling, as we drink rosé and eat goat's cheese and olives out by the orchard. It feels very *Call Me by Your Name* staying with you in this grand old house with its stone walls and high arched windows through which light floods in the late afternoon. I learn here the pain of policing myself, because the thought of making you feel uncomfortable fills me with shame so intense, I am silenced.

Until one day, you tell me excitedly you have a boyfriend, and I am happy for you, because I love you.

Then there is *you,* who I meet later that same year. You and I share secrets in the library, side glances and wanting smiles. We walk home together one afternoon and stand outside Tesco talking for three hours until it's dark all around us. You had wanted to buy peanut butter and now the store is closing, so you kiss me on the cheek and rush inside. I ride home as sleet begins to fall from the sky, knuckles burning in the cold.

You say you have feelings for me, but you have a boyfriend across the ocean, and he is waiting for you, and you tell me you're going to go. I learn the blue edge of almost kisses.

Two years later, you write to me to tell me you wished it had panned out differently back then and I feel the acute rush of that yearning all over again, even after all this time.

Then there is *you* whose hand I don't hold in public, even though I yearn to, because I don't feel safe on this street. And *you* who I don't want to kiss in front of certain people, even though I desperately want to, because they continue to make jokes about gay people that crush me inside out. And *you* and *you* and *you,* who for one reason or another, we cannot be, or we cannot become.

When I paint, I often paint with haste. *Finished!* I'll shout, as if it were a race. The decision to go back to the work, I feel, is a brave one. Because the painting gets richer in the retelling, in the reworking, in the addition of layers and the deepening of the colours.

With love, it is easy, too, I think, to shout, *Finished, I'm DONE!* It is easy to become hardened by heartache, to become closed off and guarded. The decision to go back to love, then, is a brave one. Because the heart gets richer in the retelling, in the reworking, in the addition of new lovers and the deepening of the story.

To sit within the blue of yearning, and to turn, always, back to love – that is how I remain soft, for me, and for you.

Sincerely

Dylin

Dylin Hardcastle: writer, artist, Provost scholar and research assistant at Oxford University

Dear Lover

Do you believe in angels?

One sad, lonesome day, I asked my mum up above
To look down on me, send me someone to love.
Help me find my direction, a new path to pursue,
I know she was listening because then there was you.

The broken roads I have travelled have led to here
You were following behind me, that's now pretty clear.
You're the major to my minor, the sharp to my flat.
You're the beat in my heart, there's no doubt about that.

You're the Yin to my Yang, they say opposites attract
Yet we're exactly the same, so go figure that.
You're the wise to my foolish, the day to my night.
How did she know how to get it just right?

Let's hold hands and travel this road together
With our hearts always open, no matter the weather.

Our minds always full of wisdom and affection
And our feet always facing the right direction.

Thank you for the wonderful human being that you are.
For loving me and blessing my life so far.
As long as we live, I'll always believe
That angels exist and mine sent you to me.

What took you so long?

Love always

Lyndy 💟

*Lyndel Murphy: composer with a four-decade career as a vocalist
and musician (*The Shania TWAIN Show, Australia)

Dear Lover

My chest, it rises like a swelling ocean. And you. You sleep beside me without movement, without yet knowing that this is how it all begins for us.

Yesterday, as we sat under the sun, our skin folded together, blended in with the sand. White on white on white against the horizon-blue. Look at us there, sitting together. At the end of the day, with our towels hanging from our shoulders, looking out as the sunset held on. Look at us, our knees touching. Our toes in the cooling sand as the first night winds started to brush up against our skin.

Look. At. Us. Here. Now, under the first shatterings of the new-day-sunlight, with my dress hanging on the chair near the door, with your half-finished beer on the windowsill and the soft breeze acting as a quiet symphony written to hold us in this moment. Hold. You. Look at you as I turn towards you. I hear you sigh, feel your body move backwards and press onto my chest. Look at you. At us. At this. This beginning. Our reflective light. And. I measure the held distance between us with my tide-breath. In. Out. In, and all the way out until it touches the small hairs on the back of your neck. You wake, stir, and. I am sticky. My crotch smells. It is full of copper and the sour of you. I place my chin on the back of your neck, lay with you like a darling. Here. You turn. Look at me. Ask me the name of the bay we visited yesterday. *Neptune,* I say, *where the ocean meets the river.* I kiss your lips. And. We. Are becoming the swells, the breaking waves near the shoreline. The rising of a crest.

Mandy

Mandy Beaumont: award-winning writer, academic and book reviewer concerned with the reading and writing of philosophically engaged fiction

Dear Lover

I've been thinking a lot about making recently and how grateful I am to have someone to share this passion with.

I can't quite pinpoint how that all started – something to do with Grandpa's shed smelling of sawdust and petrol and the dollhouse and rocking chair he made for me when I was little. And when I was a little older, I would sit at the kitchen table at my grandparents' house with glitter glue and make Christmas cards for everyone I knew. Older still I made paper flowers, and for a school project I made my own toy with plenty of help – a butterfly with wheels – after studying a book called *Making Toys That Move*. I became a frequent friend of the hot glue gun until my love of words grew so large that I spent all my spare time writing, at least until I realised how related making and writing were.

I was never an inventor or all that good with handiwork really. To me, making something is about more than just the gift itself or the stubbornness of choosing to make from scratch instead of buying something new. It's about making the time to see through a project for someone I care about and thinking about the way they'd like it.

It shouldn't surprise me that our first date was all about making too. I'm so glad we made balloon animals that day. It was exhilarating, sitting close enough to touch and see you in all your alluring detail while nearly failing to follow the instructions for the balloon bear – so many complicated twists that it kept coming undone. Our eyes meeting before that first kiss was the beginning of something special, and I knew I was totally falling for you when not long later you made me even more balloon flowers for our lockdown Valentine's Day. I cherish your needle felting and the ukulele you painted for me (even if I haven't really learnt how to play it yet!) and the time you made mini croissant cereal for me because I got a bit too obsessed with seeing it online.

I love that sometimes your sunnies live in the glass bowl I blew for you in the shape of your favourite bucket hat, and that you take my hand-bound book with you to watercolour in when you're away for work. I appreciate and feel so loved and understood when you make something that couldn't be for anyone but me – a needle-felted banana blowing glass. I could cry. I may not quite share your enthusiasm for Meatloaf, but I will always remember the effort you put into making a PowerPoint presentation on why *Bat Out of Hell* is the greatest album of all time. Every moment with you is making a commitment to continuing to love and understand each other. I love nothing more than making you laugh, especially when you least expect it. And I love making pizza with you, because as we all know, you used to work in a pizza shop.

I look forward to our future of making – activities we've already talked about like giant board games and homemade ice cream. But also to making music, jokes, dinners, memories, love, a family, friends and happiness. I love you and I love making a life together.

Love

Nani/Clareadactyl de Lune/Clare Force One

Clare Millar: writer, books editor at The Big Issue, *bookseller at Readings and responsible for so many reputable bylines that even her parents are proud*

Dear Lover

I'm so terribly sorry that things didn't work out between us. Though I'd like you to know that I've spent a great deal of time trying to understand the reasons we're not still together. I'm pretty sure it had nothing to do with the complete lack of (needless to say) sex, nor – come to think of it – anything else that could be categorised as physical intimacy. We certainly never kissed, although, thinking back, I may have hugged you once. I remember holding your hand when we sat on the big green bench near the bins, though I think I was just admiring the bandaid on your finger where your cat had bitten you after you'd tried to put her out the window to see if she would land on all four legs. (I never asked. Did she?)

I remember you had the most wonderful car coat. I had never heard of a car coat, and certainly didn't have one myself, but I recall it being a fine powder blue colour, and you told me it was a special coat that could only be worn when riding in the car, or when drinking milk. That impressed me no end. I lobbied my parent hard for such a car coat but no dice, I'm afraid.

I'm pretty sure you were the love of my life, or at least could have been. What is without question, however, is that ours remains the purest and most uncomplicated relationship I have ever had, and if we had just stuck at it, given it a go, I'm certain I would have avoided the monotonous procession of hurt and failure, betrayal and mistrust that was to follow me for the next 53 years.

And I may well have ended up with a truly wonderful car coat.

Michael

Michael Veitch: well-known author, actor and ABC TV and radio presenter

Dear Lover

I've dreamt of you since I was conscious enough to want something. Something that I longed for, was excited by, was challenged by and, at times, afraid of.

What would a love demand of me? What was I willing to give it? If I gave all of myself to you, as young girls are told we must, what's left for me?

The idea of 'love' was a mix of fantasy, the ultimate wish fulfilment, impossible romantic gestures, lust, deep passion and excitement.

Then my first crushes were an eclectic mix of a young Donald Sutherland, Malcolm McDowell, Daniel Day-Lewis, Peter Garrett, Rick Wakeman and Predator ... yes, the alien.

When I finally started dating at the late age of 21 (my back brace put the brakes on, something I'm quite grateful for, actually) it was an interesting wake-up call. There was indeed passion, lust and excitement, friendship, even a bit of romance. But there was also misunderstandings, arguments, boredom, manipulation and jealousy.

I realised I didn't always like who I was in a relationship, I wasn't always the best version of myself. I was disappointed in my behaviour and decided I had to try to reconcile who I was when I embarked on a relationship.

I also tolerated bad behaviour from some of my partners and could not for the life of me understand why I let myself be disrespected and taken for granted. And at times jealousy crept into the equation, something I never understood and could not abide.

A bit of therapy, a few more failed attempts, whilst meeting some remarkable men along the way, and also learning to recognise the odd sociopath/narcissist (nice). I eventually embarked on a marriage. And it's still chugging along to this day :). So, dear Lover, to whom do I refer to when I say this? Well ... I reckon it's me ;). Lover, love, loving. What infinite gifts these are that we give ourselves. Self-love which ends up enhancing the love I have to share. I love my husband, my family, my remarkable friends. And the love of my life, my daughter.

Dear Lover, what a RIDE this is.

Love

George xxx

Georgie Parker: acclaimed actor, Australian treasure and beloved person

Dear Lover

Firstly, quickly, Sylvie, I need to let you know that this is for you and not another 'Lover'.

I didn't want you to have to read five paragraphs before I said the word 'Sylvie', thinking 'Dear Lover' might be for Shaneequa or Crystal or Destiny or Bambi or Cinnamon.

Also, if you find 'top ten stripper names' in my Google search history it was to find the names for the line above. I promise.

Sylvie, I've been waiting for this opportunity, waiting for a chance, this moment, to let you know that while the flowers I buy you from the servo are sweet (or are they?) and the Westfield gift vouchers I buy you when I can't think of what else to buy you are thoughtful (or are they?), there's so much more to you, to us. And I now have this wonderful opportunity to put it in black and white.

The good times, and there are plenty, are easy and fun, but it's the tough times, the heavier, complicated, more complex moments where you show your superhuman powers.

From the moment I first saw you I had a tingling sensation, not like when you catch a cold sore on a Contiki tour tingling sensation, but like when your heart skips a beat and you momentarily lose your breath.

Your blue eyes, Bora Bora lagoon-at-low-tide super-neon-blue eyes, hypnotised me then and still do 30 years on, every time I look at you.

Those beautiful eyes, a window to your beautiful soul, can make me do anything. They can make me laugh, they can make me cry, they can make me stack the dishwasher properly, they can even make me put the toilet seat down and pick up my socks from the bedroom floor, that's how incredibly powerful they are. Most importantly they constantly deliver warmth and love into my world and the worlds of everyone around you.

You are one of a kind and I feel blessed that you're mine, and I'm sorry about the socks on the floor right now but I was too busy writing this letter to my lover to pick them up.

XX L

Larry 'The Price is Right' *Emdur: multi-nominee for 'The Most Popular' everything, previous host of anything that's ever been aired, ex-newsreader from everywhere and one of Australia's best-known faces as the host of* The Morning Show

Dear Lover

A share-house party, eighteen years ago. I was high or drunk or both. All bad decisions and no tomorrows.

You were in the background, the shadows – we saw each other.

Your friends warned you, and maybe you should've listened. But you sensed something between us – something more than hints of a damaged future.

In a room above a shop in Carlton, nights without sleep. Neighbours write polite letters about how they *can't take much more*. Police at the door downstairs. Mood swings, hallucinations, other imperfections.

You made us soup. It was delicious.

Somehow, we came out the other side. You steered us away from the rocks, but still I drifted towards them.

Shakespeare wrote about love a fair bit. Maybe too much. But he said when found anew, it can be made into something stronger.

For us, it's made of small things. It's reality TV and coffee in bed. It's handmade pottery and chicken schnitzels. It's dreams of a place somewhere.

It isn't fancy gifts, lavish trips or florid declarations. It's seven houses, six cars, two dogs and never (ever) any cats.

It's simple. It's ordinary. It's miraculous.

x Mark

Mark Brandi: bestselling author and winner of the coveted British Crime Writers' Association Debut Dagger award

Acknowledgements

To all of our wonderful contributors – thank you for your time, for your brainwords and for donating your letters free of charge. Thank you to Shaun Tan for our critters, to Vanessa Radnidge for her continued guidance, to Chris Maddigan and Annie Carroll for always being there, and kudos to Sooz Camilleri, Clare Millar, Helen Townsend, Penelope Bartlau, Sophie Hamley and Brooke Davis for helping me gather contributors. Thank you to Rebecca Allen and Graeme Jones. Massive gratitude to Lucy Freeman, the real editor of this book, for her expert stewardship. And thank you, of course, to all the lovers. Without you there would be no letters!

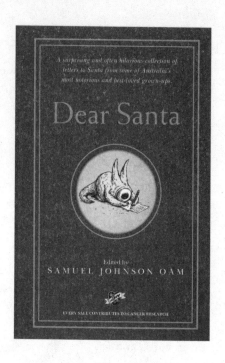

If you could ask Santa for absolutely anything, what
would you ask for? *Dear Santa* is a collection of letters
to Santa from some of Australia's most notable
notables and best-loved grown-ups, including
Helen Garner, Adam Hills, Deborah Mailman,
Rove McManus, Leigh Sales, Grant Denyer, Molly
Meldrum, Shaun Micallef, Missy Higgins and many
more. *Surprising, entertaining, wicked and witty, this
little book of letters is the perfect gift for your favourite
human.*

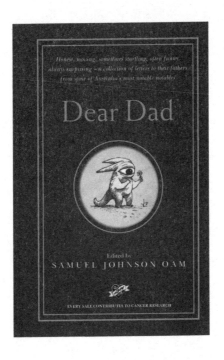

Dear Dad

Edited by
SAMUEL JOHNSON OAM

EVERY SALE CONTRIBUTES TO CANCER RESEARCH

If you could tell your dad anything, what would
it be? *Dear Dad* is an honest, moving, emotionally
memorable collection of letters to their fathers from
some of Australia's most notable notables, including
Steve Waugh, Trent Dalton, Samuel Johnson, Kathy
Lette, John Williamson, Susie Youssef, Michala
Banas, Glenn Shorrock, Joel Creasey, Shannon
Noll, Michelle Law, Ben Gillies and many more.
*This heartfelt, honest and very human book of letters will
make you smile and make you cry. It is the perfect gift for
the dad in your life.*

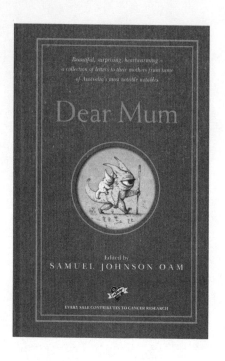

If you could tell your mum anything, what would
it be? *Dear Mum* is a beautiful, surprising and
heartwarming collection of letters to their mothers
from some of Australia's most notable notables,
including Amanda Keller, Vika and Linda Bull, Guy
Pearce, Elizabeth Tan, Rebecca Gibney, Peter Helliar,
Clare Wright, Hilde Hinton, Gillian O'Shaughnessy,
Adam Spencer, Brooke Davis, Lawrence Mooney,
Patti Newton, Shane Jacobson, Julie Koh, Susie
Youssef, Lehmo, Favel Parrett, Matilda Brown and
many more. *This whole-hearted, warm and emotional
assembly of letters is the perfect gift for the mum in your life.*

If you would like to find out more about Hachette Australia,
our authors, upcoming events and new releases you can visit
our website or our social media channels:

hachette.com.au

HachetteAustralia
HachetteAus

loveyoursister.org

Love Your Sister is Australia's hardest working cancer
vanquishing charity.

Join Sam's 1000 here: